Adding the E:
Perspectives of Grief Through
Recounts, Letters, and Poetry

Adding the E:
Perspectives of Grief Through Recounts, Letters, and Poetry

Arielle Sokoll-Ward

Inara Publishing

An Imprint of GCRR Press
1312 17th Street Suite 549
Denver, CO 80202

INFO@GCRR.ORG • INARAPUBLISHING.COM

Inara Publishing
An imprint of GCRR Press
1312 17th Street Suite 549
Denver, CO 80202
www.inarapublishing.com

*Some names have been changed to protect people's identities.

Typesetter/Copyeditor/Proofreader: Allison Guy
Cover Design: Angie Alaya
Front Cover Image: Arielle Sokoll-Ward
Back Cover Headshot Photographer: Lauren Leon

Library of Congress Cataloging-in-Publication Data

Adding the e : perspectives of grief through recounts, letters, and poetry   /
Arielle Sokoll-Ward
p.   cm.
Includes bibliographic references (p.).
ISBN (Print): 978-1-7378469-7-0
ISBN (eBook): 978-1-7378469-6-3
1. Grief.   2. Loss (Psychology).   3. Bereavement—Psychological aspects.   4. Life change events.   5. Love   I. Title.

BF575.G7   .S656   2022

☙

To the people who showed up for me and continue to show up for me.

And to my siblings: Nathan, Kyla, Nediva, and Jadon.

There isn't anyone else who I would let make fun of me the way you all do.
And there isn't anyone else I laugh harder with.
You will always be my best friends and the loves of my life.

Advanced Endorsements

Arielle Sokoll-Ward has done a remarkable job of using a devastating life experience to help others. She literally emerged from the depths of grief to become a healer who now guides others through their own adversity and trauma. In this book, Arielle uses narrative, poetry, first-hand accounts, and professional expertise to share insights and hope for those who have experienced loss and for those who will—which, by the way, is all of us.

–Ron Culberson
Speaker, Author, and Former Hospice Social Worker

Look, this is a tough read. Talking honestly about raw, painful things is taboo. But that's why this book is necessary. If you have ever felt alone in your grief, you'll get words for what you've experienced here. Or if you want to understand what someone else is going through, you'll get real insight here. You don't have to read it in order if it's too much. Arielle includes her own story throughout, but sometimes, the most impactful for me were the stories others trusted her enough to share.

–Ivy Le
Host, Writer, and Producer of FOGO: Fear of Going Out

Arielle's raw and powerful sharing of her own grief journey gives us the courage to face our own challenging stories and really be here for ourselves with compassion. Feeling is the true lasting path to freedom from our wounds, and Arielle guides us there with grace, vulnerable honesty and skillful companionship.

–Erika Allison
Author of Gay the Pray Away:
Healing Your Life, Love, and Relationships
from the Harms of LGBT Conversion Therapy

Profoundly raw and honest book about love, grief, and healing. In *Adding the E: Perspectives of Grief through Recounts, Letters, and Poetry*, Arielle extends a deeply personal invitation into her own life-altering loss and journey as well as the journey of others. The book eloquently captures the inexplicable pain that is born from loss. From a place of real vulnerability, Arielle shares how the process of healing from grief can come from moments of clarity - and sometimes even joy - to honor the life lost and those left behind.

–Saman Akhtar, MS/MBA

Arielle Sokoll-Ward's *Adding the E* is the gut-wrenching and raw, yet painfully beautiful tribute that you didn't know you needed in your life. Trust me - you do. Her pure, unfiltered words dig beneath the surface and allow the reader to experience the gritty, evolving, and even sometimes utterly delightful emotions Arielle felt as she grieved for the loss of her companion and beyond. Worth a read, and then worth sharing with others.

–Mikki J. Gates, SHRM-SCP
TEDxManitouSprings Curator and Escape Room Addict

In a portrait of deep, startling grief, we are taken by the hand through someone's darkest days. Arielle bravely and vividly shows us the ripple effects of trauma with each story, letter, and memory shared. *Adding the E* is a testament to the resiliency, beauty, and debilitating heartbreak of being a human bonded to another through love and loss. Through this powerful lens, it is hard not to also be struck by how we could better show up for those around us who are facing their own journeys with grief.

–Danielle E. Cochran
COO, Quality of Life Care, LLC
End-of-Life Advocate

Contents

Preface

During the summer of 2015, I met Hannah for the first time to go to outdoor yoga at Boston Street Pier Park in Baltimore. We started doing this as a way to increase the joy and self-care in our lives during what had been the hardest year of my life. After yoga, we walked over to Starbucks to caffeinate and started to talk about Drew. Though he wasn't the only topic of our conversation, he of course took the spotlight, as he was the one who had brought us together.

Hannah and Drew had known each other long before Drew and I had even met. She had been someone who reached out and showed up for me, even though she and I barely knew each other before Drew passed. After the fact, she accompanied me when I wanted to go to Drew's home group Alcoholics Anonymous meeting to feel connected to him. I remember the intense fear I had going back to the building where I had last gone with Drew in support of him and his recovery. Would I be welcomed? Would I be triggering others? Would I completely lose it myself? Her extension of kindness reached further than I could have imagined; others gathered to support me in my grief—in all of our grief. Sitting with me in solidarity and comfort as I either painfully sobbed or remained callously numb through the handful of meetings we attended together. Holding my hand as others in the community approached me with benevolent words about Drew.

That particular day at Starbucks, sugary drinks in hand, we were talking about the letters that I had been writing on a nightly basis for months. Hannah asked me if one day I would publish these letters, maybe in a book. I remember being intrigued by the zest of such vulnerability being made public. Going back to that moment, I now think that the original excitement came from a place of wanting recognition, thinking that sharing myself in this way would be inspiring, a distinct act that others would dream of doing. Though I still hope to be inspiring to others, I believe I am now in a more altruistic place to honor this time in my life and to honor Drew. Through years of experiencing and embracing my own grief, as well as holding space for others in theirs, I have included parts of these letters in lectures, performances, and a TEDx talk. I now return to that conversation in 2015 and say yes. I have chosen to share a selection of the letters I wrote to Drew, in their integrity, within this book, finally bringing to life a fantasy that was envisioned years before, though now, the intention of sharing these with others has greatly changed. It lines up with the same intention I have when I do the work that I love to do as a therapist. My intention is to show the humanity in grief, the collectiveness in loss, and the resiliency in love.

Introduction

It started with a loss, a tremendous loss that impacted me from every angle and destroyed every part of my being. This same loss has led me to live a life of purpose and gratitude, finding the strength hidden within heartbreak. A plot twist originating in bravery turned me into a grief therapist, curious about others' experiences with grief and loss.

What you are about to read is the final product of that curiosity. I collected qualitative research using one simple five-word prompt: "Tell me about your grief."

What I got back was breathtaking, heartbreaking, and real. These were perspectives and stories of people grieving, losing, and gaining. Some responses were literal and to the point, others were colorfully painted words of emotion, and a handful were even funny.

You will see conclusions and theme interpretations about the responses I received. These responses come from nine states within the United States as well three different countries. Ages of the respondents range from twenty-four to sixty-seven years old and are representative of gender throughout the spectrum. I have pulled direct statements from the participants that I feel especially support these conclusions. All direct quotes are with permission of the participant to be used in this book.

Supporting the responses from the research, I share some of my clients' experiences and insights within the narrative. These, too, are with permission and to maintain confidentiality. The names have been changed.

You will also notice that there are letters throughout Part One of the book. These letters were written in a time where grief consumed most of my being. To keep the authenticity of the emotion felt at the time of creation, the letters themselves have not been edited past changing four of the names mentioned to pseudonyms. These were written to Drew. If you happen to be someone who didn't know Drew, and this book has ended up in your hands, thank you. He would feel famous.

Lastly, the poetry. Poetry has been my creative outlet for years, especially in times of consuming grief. These pieces were written between the years of 2013 and 2021 on multiple subjects. However, they all have one thing in common: they were created in efforts to heal.

My Commitment to the Reader

Everything in this book is true. True emotion, true stories. For those who have asked to remain anonymous, I have used a pseudonym within the writing. I have tried my best to be the most authentic and real version of myself in order to convey an honest look at grief and loss. A sincere truth about how I and others experience it. What is written in these pages is wholeheartedly me ...

And you.

And us.

Part One: My Grief

You will never know how grateful I am to know you are reading this.

Have you ever read something you wrote years ago?

There is no other time-traveling experience like it.

6:20 a.m.

Shanghai, China

I find something familiar and walk in.

"What time do you open?"

"7:00."

"Thank you. What time is it?"

She counts on her fingers. "One, two, three, four, five. Five."

"5:00?"

She nods her head; I walk out. 5:00 a.m. in Shanghai's airport. It's cold and quiet. Eerie, almost. But it's colder downstairs where my gate is, so I'm roaming the top floor. I never thought I would ever go to China. But I remember as a kid always wanting to because there was nothing in the world that was better than Chinese food. My views have since changed. But I guess this wasn't exactly my choice. Flying fourteen or so hours from JFK to arrive in Shanghai to watch the sunrise and walk the terminal with a few other traveling strangers.

I go into another store and ask, "Do you take Visa?"

Trying to ignore the loud voice in my head that is saying I'm a privileged white girl, assuming that other people will understand me.

It has a point.

"Okay," she replies.

I want to get a drink and some authentic Chinese snack because my head is pounding. I end up going with a Chinese version of Pringles, a white chocolate Dove bar, and a pineapple/apple juice to wash it down. At least the juice was something I hadn't had before. Too afraid to venture too much because I can't read the ingredients and if wheat is in whatever I'm about to eat, it will be a terrible, regrettable plane ride. The woman tells me my total in Chinese, and I hand her my credit card. I have no idea how much I paid for breakfast. Bon appétit.

I sit and write and read a book of poetry. I watch employees open their shops. I watch as locals, westerners, even monks pass by (from the look of it). I wait my four-hour layover until 8:10 a.m., when I get on another plane for four hours and continue on to Bangkok. My stomach feels weird, and normally I would be worried it was what I ate, but I have been feeling this way for the past couple of hours. Probably just nerves, excitement, the new air. The flight information next to me shows many romantic and exotic destinations: Rome, Tokyo, Singapore, Chiang Mai, Amsterdam, Paris, Moscow, Dubai … Detroit. Well, maybe not every destination.

Airports are a weird thing. They remind me of casinos in a way. Though a casino is built with a different agenda in mind, you still kind of don't know where you are. Casinos are built with no clocks or windows; airport terminals and runways look very similar to each other. Looking outside, you can rarely tell where you are in the area, even the world. And even with all of the Chinese script around me, I still feel like there is no way I could be in China. Everyone in here has their own agenda, excitement, or maybe even dread. Everyone is going somewhere, physically. Romantic or not. It's an interesting feeling walking around here, being so noticeably foreign and different. I'm not used to it.

Privilege.

I don't know what to expect on this trip to Thailand, and I hope to keep it that way. Whatever the case or outcome may be, I feel like it is going to be really great. It even has me writing again.

It's bright

The sky has opened up

It always seems to do that when I visit you

I'm laying out, always on top of you

Staring at your name

I come here to feel whole

It's impossible because you are forever this hole that was dug for you

And I'm trying not to sink in my own

I'm trying not to think about how many hours have passed

While I am out living a life that should have been ours

The fantasy that remains in the past

13,012

Those are the hours without you

Those are the hours that I have occupied alone

And the hours that I've been stuck in bygone days

Still wondering why this happened to you

Why did this happen to me

Thinking of the person that you should be

Tell me

What should I have done

What could I have done

The horrible things I would do to hear you say you love me one last time

Because I didn't think you would do it one last time

It was your last time

You put that needle in your arm

How can something I never touched destroy my life

You used heroin so I could add the E

The heroin that you chose is the heroine that is now me

I remember to say your name

Friday, August 7, 2015

12:34 a.m.

Dear Drew,

Five months. Today was one of the saddest days I have had in a really long time. I pretty much just cried all the time in therapy. Also in the car, a lot. I kept it together for the kids I babysat. They were trying to break the world record for the longest Uno game. It was cute. They said, "love you" as I was leaving. Adorable. Erin told me to go home and curl up in the comforter and just feel everything, cry my eyes out. I don't know what it is, but I don't feel like I have to cry right now. I miss you a fuck ton, though. I feel like today, I wasn't living or even existing but surviving. I survived today, and honestly if that's all I could do, that is good enough for me. I know there have been a lot of days like that, and there will be a lot more. I sometimes feel like five months have gone by in a flash, and other days, it feels like a lifetime with everything I have gone without. I was wondering if the time passes or if it just disappears. I don't know some days. A lot of the time, I have no memory of full conversations or events or days. It kind of freaks me out, but I know that's a normal part of grief. I wish I were going through this with you, though. Having you next to me as someone I could talk to and lean on and love during this time would be really great. But I have myself. And my friends and family. But mostly myself. I feel like I do that intentionally, but that's okay. I think sometimes this is something I need to figure out on my own. I think I am going to go to the gym tomorrow. I should have done it today. I have been trying to go more, knowing you would say something like, "Get it, girl" or "Did you murder it?" So, sometimes I say that to myself on your behalf. I texted Denise from Michael's today to check on your shirt ... another unhelpful answer. It's been five months, and they haven't put it up. That is unacceptable to me. So, if it doesn't go up soon, I told her I want it. I'll frame it and put it up in my room. Or maybe give it to your parents. I don't know. But I sure as hell know I'm not going to let it sit in a box. You would be proud of my assertiveness. So, I thought even though it was really little, I would at least try to do something about that today to honor you. I miss you, baby, every second of every day. That's never going to change. Stay with me. Look after me. Be beside me.

I love you more and more,

Arielle

1

Happy Birthday,

Happy Anniversary

It's February 8, 2014, and I'm twenty-three years old. Like all good millennial love stories, it started with brunch. A group of girlfriends and I who worked at a restaurant uptown in Towson, Maryland gathered that Saturday at Michael's Café, a staple establishment in the Towson/Timonium area. It was one of the girls' birthdays, and mimosas were a birthday requirement. We sat down at the bar, where another one of the girls' winter flings was working. Soon after placing our drink order, the bar packed, and we were moved to a round corner booth nearby. Unfortunately for my friend, her fling was getting served with that brunch rush, quickly becoming weeded and therefore unable to continue to be our server.

Up walked our new server, drinks in hand, who had a side of fresh meat next to him—the trainee. He was in a bad mood, quick on his feet, wasn't very friendly, and didn't make much eye contact. À la, the "too busy for your bullshit" waiter. One of my friends who is originally from the Towson area started talking to him and later told us that he was a long-time friend and even her junior prom date in high school. I told the group of gals how cute I think he is, and my friends encouraged me to go for it and lay on some charm. The next time he came back to the table, I started to hit on him … which didn't go well. My friend then told us that he and I go to the same church. I looked at her, knowing exactly what she was doing and that she thought she was being funny because she knows I'm Jewish.

I then looked at him and asked, "Are you Jewish?"

He nodded.

Anxiety must have taken over because the next thing I said still makes me roll my eyes at myself to this day.

"What's your favorite Jewish holiday? Mine's Sukkot because I like getting drunk in the sukkah!"

This is a lie, and I have no idea why I said it. I don't particularly have a fondness for Sukkot, and I have definitely never gotten drunk in a sukkah. Is this my idea of a flirtatious humble brag? Yikes.

He gave a half-assed laugh and walked away.

I turned back around, and my friend looked at me like I'd lost my mind. Her voice lowered into a loud whisper and a shockingly sassy tone. "Oh my God, he's in recovery! You can't say things like that to him!"

Wow. I blew it.

Throughout the rest of the meal, we casually made eye contact, but I no longer trusted my pick-up skills. We got our checks, mine a whopping fourteen dollars—I think he hooked the table up. I left a fifty percent tip, trying to apologize in the only appropriate server-to-server manner. As my friends paid their checks, I excused myself and called my grandpa to wish him a happy birthday as well. When I got back, I decided that my tragic pick-up line wasn't going to stop me from giving this server my number. But as I approached the table again to my friends gathering their things, I was handed a piece of paper. My *very funny* friend told me that she got his number for me. I told her that I was planning on giving it to him myself, and I didn't want him to think that I needed her to do this for me! I wanted him to know that I'm a strong, independent, self-sufficient woman who can give her phone number out herself! I looked down at the handwritten paper with the "443" area code and his name.

Drew.

They say when a writer loves you, you can never die

We have both lived many lives before meeting up in this one

And the space between your shoulders

That is where I want to live

I, just like many others, am familiar with monumental losses. The day I met Drew was a day that will forever stay in my mind. In a way, it was the day that set the tone for what seems to be the most dynamic part of my life, thus far. After meeting that afternoon at Michael's Café, we scheduled a date four days later. We both thought the other lived close to Michael's, so when he offered to pick me up and my address was in Baltimore City, about a mile and a half from where he also lived, it of course seemed a little like fate. The day we met, I had straightened my very long reddish-brown hair. So, when he picked me up and my curls were flowing like the Jewess that I am, I remember the shocked look on his face. This made such an impact that when I first met Drew's parents, *they* told me about this moment. It was February, so naturally, it was snowing. We changed dinner plans and decided to go to an eclectic diner that was only a few blocks away from my house. Papermoon Diner is a Baltimore City gem; ask anyone. I had a Caesar salad wrap, and Drew had a milkshake—along with a large meal that I'm sure he inhaled. This would be the first of many milkshakes he would order in our relationship and one of my favorite things about him.

The date continued as we headed back to his house. I quickly realized the snow was getting heavier, and I was not in the mood to be stuck at this home that looked like it belonged in a creepy horror movie. So, I suggested we head back to mine. We were snowed in together for forty-eight hours thanks to the great blizzard of 2014. During this time, it felt like we nosedived deep into each other's lives. We were intimately vulnerable and created a deep connection in a short amount of condensed time. Drew would later tell me that he knew he loved me that night of our first date. Due to the intense beginning of our relationship, we coined February 12 as our anniversary, which seemed fitting since he was already in love. Our road hit some bumps, and we were each tested with our own versions of grief and loss as individuals and as a couple. But our love and infatuation with each other was all-consuming. Two people who were impassioned in what has felt like a once-in-a-lifetime kind of love.

This once-in-a-lifetime love most certainly caused a once-in-a-lifetime type of grief. As I learned that first night, Drew was in recovery from not only substances but a tumultuous life caused by those substances. He was part of a tight-knit recovery community that he helped create and sustain with his willingness to help and, at times, save others. These qualities trickled into other parts of his life, only making him a more selfless, helpful, and kind person. Knowing this about someone only validates how confusing and horrific it is when urge overwhelms recovery, and they fall back into addiction.

On March 6, 2015, Drew overdosed on heroin and died alone in his bedroom. The following comes from the eulogy given at Drew's funeral.

We learned everything there was to know about each other in that time. That was the time when he told me about his past and the demons on his shoulders, and I told him about mine. I remember thinking, he seems like he could be a hard person to love sometimes, but I really hoped that I would be able to make that decision for myself in the future. The truth is, Drew was and still is my absolute true love. His loving, compassionate, and considerate nature, among other things, made him more than human. He has shown me comfort in times I didn't deserve and was always there for me and loved me at some of the hardest times in my life. Through all of this and more, he made it incredibly easy and fun to love him. Soon after we first met, I invited him over to make homemade ravioli. Although I think I'm a good cook, I messed up on the recipe. After maybe five minutes of eating, I finally said, "I don't know what you think, but this is gross." He dropped his fork and with a breath of relief said, "I'm so glad you said something. This is disgusting. I can't eat this anymore." And if he were here to tell this story, he would then go on, in detail, about how bad it actually was.

Before I met Drew, I remember asking God for something or someone to help me because I was in need of true help. Then, Drew showed up. I don't think he knew it then, but I hope he learned that he really saved me, and I only wish I could have saved him back. We stood by each other through the really good and the really bad because, as we would say, "Your problems are my problems, and my problems are your problems." I wish we could keep saying that because I would have done anything for him because he was everything to me. He was an incredibly resilient person and a constant inspiration for me to be better than I was. Drew and I spoke and fantasized about the future we would have together and what our plans were. He was my plan. When we would talk about marriage, I always had this picture in my head of me walking down the aisle to him, with Brad, Noah*, Tyler*, and Diggs standing strong behind him. I think he was more excited to have kids than to get married because he would always say how good of a dad he would be. He spoke about how his father was the perfect example of how a man should be. He not only hoped he would be that to his child one day, but he strived to be that man every day. He was everything I could have asked for in a man. He accepted me for things that I had trouble accepting in myself. He understood and cared when I thought no one else would. He was an absolutely extraordinarily smart and kind individual that I feel honored to call my love, my partner, and my best friend. I am grateful that I can call his friends and family my friends and family, and I was welcomed and accepted into his circle. We shared so many adventures together with so much laughter and happiness. He made everything better. We made each other better by being together because we were unapologetically ourselves when we were with each other.

The grief I experienced, specifically in the first year, was in many ways parallel to the love we had for each other: all-consuming, impassioned, and unlike anything I've ever known. Whether I felt ready or not, I was thrown into my grief headfirst. Almost unable to hide it or stuff it down, it was often seeping out of me in a very outwardly emotional way. For many years, I felt like this day of extraordinary loss would define who I was, and to some extent that has been true. But what I have found to be even more authentic was thinking about the hopeful feeling I had the day Drew and I first met. Eagerly waiting to see him again, wondering about the possibilities to come. I have learned to hold the same wonder with my grief and the grief people share with me. Wondering how long the grief journey will be, who we will become, and what we will gain.

What my sister taught me:

I am terrified that I am forgetting you

Why can't I remember the sound of your heartbeat

Or the sound the stairs made when you ran down because you were late

When you died, who I was died too

She said we go through many rebirths

When a relationship ends, a death happens, or a trauma takes place

We mourn who we once were

I mourn who I was when I was with you

She isn't here

The difference between you and I is that when I died, there was a rebirth

I was a bud, now flourishing into resilience, into the resistance

I flourish because I have done this many times before

I have had many rebirths since your death

And even though it seems impossible to do it again, I will.

And even though it seems impossible to survive again, I will.

2

Ego Death

It's 9:30 a.m. when I get the call.

"I need your help. He's not moving. I don't know what to do. You need to get over here."

It's his roommate. Though we are friends, we aren't the friends that call each other. But for some reason, when I saw his name come up on my phone, I wasn't surprised.

Like I was expecting it and ready to answer.

I'm stuck.

Snow is on the ground, and my car is a piece of shit in the snow.

A million things are going through my mind.

Should I shower? I should shower. No, there's no time.

But I should brush my teeth.

I'm staring at my phone, waiting for a call back, anxiously dreading it.

He calls. I stop breathing.

"I'm really sorry to tell you this, but … "

… your life is about the change forever

… you will not see him today

… your plans just went up into flames

… your marriage to him is no longer happening

… your kids together won't be born

… your life is about to crumble to the ground

You won't know why.

"I'm really sorry to tell you this, but Drew passed away this morning."

I stop breathing. I can't breathe.

I can't breathe.

I fall to the ground, screaming, crying.

A total loss of control that I have never felt before.

I am debilitated to the ground, as my biggest support in this world cannot hold me up any longer.

A movie comes to mind for a second.

This must be what it feels like to be in a movie.

This can't be real life.

My life was with him—my plan was with him.

The way I fell and screamed was only something I had seen in the movies.

I need someone to yell cut!

Please, someone, yell cut!

No one did.

A memory that now lives in my body.

Acceptance isn't a word I know yet——and I don't want to get to know it.

Survival is what I know.

I will survive the pain, so he feels none.

Drew would tell me, "An addict's mind is always in survival mode."

So, I know he was just trying to do the same thing.

Survive.

That is what I do. That is who I am.

I will do it now for both of us.

Because when your soulmate dies ...

Their soul survives in you.

Thinking back to that day is visceral. Some of the memories feel faint, while others provide me with images so vivid, it is like I am having a flashback. My mother drives me to his house in Baltimore, and I have almost no memory of the car ride. When we reach Drew's house and I get out of the car while my mom looks for a place to park, I run through the snow and swing open the door. I see people on the stairs, and I immediately run in an attempt to pass them and go up to his bedroom. The policeman catches me and tells me I can't go up there, while I am fighting to go past his arms, while the screams leave my body, and the tears roll down my face. Drew's parents and his roommate, Noah, are now at the bottom of the stairs when his roommate grabs me and pulls me down into his arms. My legs have given out, and he stands for both of us for a few moments as I cry out in anguish into his chest.

Eventually, I am walked to the living room, where we all sit for what I think is hours, but I actually have no idea. Drew's brother shows up, and so does my dad. There are only four things that I remember about this time. One: It's Friday. Earlier that week, I lent Drew money to pay a school payment. I was terrified that instead of paying the bill, he used the money, my money, to buy the heroin that would eventually kill him. While we are sitting in the living room, his dad tells me that he was able to check with the school about payments, and Drew did in fact pay that bill with the money I gave him. Two: The business side of death started very quickly. Drew's parents called the rabbi and funeral home to start making funeral plans. I can only assume this is part of the shock that his parents must have been in. A similar shock had me asking if I should shower and brush my teeth. Three: His mother asked me what Drew wanted when he died ... to be buried or cremated. I remember thinking this was such a weird thing for her to ask *me*. What may have been weirder was that I confidently knew the answer: cremation. On more than a couple of occasions, Drew told me that he wanted to be cremated, and I was the one that had to be sure he wasn't put in the ground so bugs could eat him. I would roll my eyes and sarcastically say something along the lines of, "Okay, I'll let someone know eighty years from now." Four: I heard the zipper of the body bag. Hearing the sound of a zipper so many times before. However, I know *exactly* what this zipper is for. And it's haunting.

Blank page

I have nothing

But I need something

That's why I'm here

A peek into my life

I'll show you everything, the things you will like and what you won't

The zipper, the zipper, the zipper

That's what you need to know

Ask and I'll tell

Look into the window

Look at the furniture now replaced

The walls now new

That's where love lived

That's where loved moved

My heart isn't in it

This is shit

Zip it up

I don't have any memory of the rest of the day. The days between the day Drew died and the funeral seem to be so short, yet there are memories that I have that feel like they couldn't all fit into that small amount of time. I felt grateful that his family included me in the funeral plans with the rabbi. It was important to me that the way he died was not looked over, lied about, or sugarcoated. Drew died from a heroin overdose, and I was not going to let even his family lie about that at his funeral. It would have broken his heart. The rabbi asked his parents what they wanted to do with the ashes. His mother said that maybe Drew would like them to be spread in Ocean City, a beach town that Drew had spent time in with friends. Though I can see the importance of this place and why his parents would think this would be appropriate, Ocean City just didn't feel special enough; if you have ever been to Ocean City, you know what I'm talking about. I inserted myself into the discussion and said that I really thought Drew would want his ashes spread at the Grand Canyon. He and I went on a cross-country road trip from Los Angeles to Maryland, and the Grand Canyon was one of our first stops. Drew had never been before, and showing up right at 7:00 in the evening when the sun was setting couldn't have been more perfect. Drew was very much afraid of heights and stayed away from the edge as I was basically hanging off it. With my hands on the railing, taking in the magnificent creation, I look back to see Drew sitting on a rock, gazing out into the distance. He later tells me that he had never felt more serene in his life. It's because of this memory that I knew Drew would want his ashes here. His parents agreed, and that was that.

There was a small viewing planned by his family. Beforehand, I was at Drew's house with Noah and his three other very good friends, one of them being a wonderful AA sponsor he had years back, Jack. It felt nice being included in this, as his best friend, Tyler, and I didn't get along too well. I think this was because we both have alpha personalities and were protective and felt territorial over Drew when it came to one another. But on that day, we put it aside, and we were there for each other. The guys made jokes that the next boyfriend I had had to "go through us first." It made me feel special and cared for by the people who care about Drew. We packed ourselves into one of their cars and drove to the funeral home for the viewing. I met my family, Drew's family, and close friends of theirs in the adjacent room to where the casket was.

His dad holds me, and I take a couple of deep breaths before turning my head

Anticipating seeing others who have gathered in the room—but not him

As my head turns, my eyes immediately find his painted face and combed hair

My neck snaps back, and I wail as if I had just been shot

Throwing my face in the nook of his father's shoulder

The most awful thing I have ever seen

The lifeless body of the one I love, surrendered to a casket

The gun of reality still smoking from the bullet that just made its way through my soul

Pieces of the metal still burn hot many, many sleeps later

Friday, July 24, 2015

12:21 a.m.

Dear Drew,

I think babysitting these kids is helping me become happy, or at least not as sad all the time. I have to put on a smile and be talkative and listen. And it's nice to care about something because I care about these kids. Like last night when the seven-year-old was sick, I felt like his mom, and I knew what to do because of my mom. It felt good. I went to therapy today, and it was so terrible. I only had about fifteen minutes because I had to go babysit, and I just sat there in silence. I want to curse the therapist out, and I have no idea why. I really like her; I was just so angry. I am so angry all the time, and everything makes me angry. My fuse is really short. If you were here, you would make me feel better. Talk to me about it or just hold me and let me cry or take my mind off it by making jokes. I wish you were here. There is no one to do that with. I think I am trying to do that with Jen. I really try to make her feel better as well as empathize with her and know her pain but also know that everything isn't as bad as it seems, which is weird for me to say because of how I am acting in my life right now. I don't like being angry all the time. I don't like not being a nice person. I thought I was going to be a chatterbox for fifteen minutes and then rush out, but as soon as I got in there, I was furious. She said my mom called her, which got me even more mad. I think maybe I would have said something, but after hearing that, I wasn't saying shit. She sent me an email after. Maybe I'll email her back in a couple of days. Thinking about it now gets me angry. I feel nauseous. I wonder if my secret will be online this week. Part of me wishes it is, and another part doesn't. I don't think I am capturing your death. It doesn't feel real, which is why I can function. I am angry and impulsive and feel like doing risky things. I don't even know what that means. Denise is coming to see me tomorrow. Maybe I'll feel better after talking to her. I don't even know how much I want to share with her. She is one person that I don't know if she can handle it, and I don't know if she should, and I don't want to put that feeling of pressure on her. I guess I'll play it by ear. Please be with me. In the picture of us at the Ravens game, I was looking at your hair and ears....I can still feel on my fingers the way they feel. I just want to run my fingers through your hair and down your scruffy face. Remember when I said I hope I never get used to you saying how beautiful I am? I never did. I still wish you could say it, though; I really miss it. I miss your voice and you telling me you love me. Maybe you could

stop by in my dream tonight and tell me?
Thanks, babe.

I love you, baby,

Arielle

I went back to Drew's house to talk to Noah after the viewing. We talked for a long time. I can't remember the details of this, though what I do remember was that this was the first time in my grief that I felt anger. What started as me walking to my car, "in a bad mood," turned into me screaming at the top of my lungs on the way home. That night, my mom sat beside me as I lay in bed and cried and screamed into my pillow until my throat was sore. Repeatedly saying how much I hated Drew. Saying that I didn't want to go to his funeral, and I hated him for doing this to me, for giving me this insurmountable amount of pain.

Monday, August 3, 2015

11:46 p.m.

Dear Drew,

I was pretty pissed off at you today. Sometimes, I feel like one day, I'll write to you, and I will have one frame of mind and say one thing, and then the next day, I will be doing the opposite. Such is grief; such is life; nothing makes sense. I was pissed today because you were lying to me, and I don't even know how long. I was pissed because you had twenty-four hours a day for God knows how long to tell me the truth, and you didn't, twenty-four hours a day to tell me that you were not doing well or that you relapsed or were using, and maybe if you did that, I could have fucking helped you, and maybe if I did that, you wouldn't be fucking dead, and we could be happy, and my life wouldn't be the shitshow that it fucking is every day. But maybe not. And as an addict, you self-sabotage. I know that. But it doesn't make not knowing things easier because at the moment, I am thinking that half of our relationship was a lie. I don't know anything; I am completely in the dark about something that makes no sense and something that is bringing me so much pain and that I have to live with the rest of my life. You died, and you left me here to pick up your shit and continue to live on and build back the pieces of my crumbed life. What a fucking asshole. So, yes, today I was angry. Thank God I have Noah and Denise who can pick me up and make me feel better and believe in me and will fight for me. I am angry because I don't understand this, and it's not fair, and I wish you weren't sick, and I wish you didn't lie, and I wish I could have done something. But the fact is none of that matters because whether I know the truth, which I know is impossible to know because you are the only person who knows the truth about what happened to you, it won't change the outcome. You are gone, and are not coming back, no matter how much I plead and beg you to or scream and cry; the outcome is still this. Completely heartbroken beyond repair. And that's my truth. And a part of me hates you for doing that. People can hear the pain in my voice and see it in my face when I am not putting on a front, so actually very few people. But as I was talking to Denise, I told her I want to start changing some things. About my life and about myself. I want to be more open, honest, and authentic with people. Express my vulnerability and show up for others and myself and give myself to others, while still letting people in and seeing the bruised and broken pieces of myself, while also showing them how much of a strong, bad bitch I am. So, I'm working on it. I went to yoga today; it was alright but a little slow. I'll try another class this week. I didn't talk to a stranger today, though a homeless man commented on my yoga mat, which was cool and made me smile. I wish I could have called and told you about that. The second GRASP meeting was also tonight. The same people showed up but no more. That's alright. At least they are getting help for this. I miss you. I think the anger would have processed better if you were here. I wished so bad I could call you up and yell at you, or we could have a fight, and we would yell at each other. I would give so much to even fight with you again because that means you are here, and I have an outlet. What is the outlet supposed to be when the person you are angry at is dead? I don't know.

I love you even when I hate you,

Arielle

I lost track counting the increasing casualties in my casually cruel new suit of skin

It's tight around my curves for an uncomfortably snug fit

This is definitely the wrong size, I say to myself. There must be some mistake. I must have been given this by mistake.

My body now coated in a thickened, tarred heaviness that bears the weight of my oscillating emotions

Inconvenient. Oppressive. Unconceivable.

Over time, the stiff fit becomes familiar, like my body signed an agreement to take the burden on without my consent

Flexible. Complacent. Acquired.

The skin I wear was part of the exchange

When I was forced to return the love I found, now resulting in acute loss

I was given something in return

A lackluster suit of skin that was a tangible representation of my mourning that held the parts of me together

Tradition decorated it with a black ribbon for Kriah

They didn't tell me about the day I would become protective of this skin

Fiercely protective of my grief

Scared to give it up or hang it up in the back of the dark closet

What if I need it?!

The armor I hide behind is the same one that stagnates

And this is just a rental

Soon, I will learn to shed this skin and adapt to a new, barely tailored fit

But for now, asking anyone who lays eyes on me

How do I look?

I had already written his eulogy, and in the light of day, I knew I was going to go. I wore a black dress that I had bought with him on our anniversary trip to Ocean City, in February, twelve days before he died. It was a frozen ghost town, with snow on the ground and temperatures in the twenties. We got an oceanfront room and ate our way through the weekend attempting to watch every Harry Potter movie we could pack in with a solid amount of sex breaks. It was great. When I bought the dress from the outlets located on the way to the beach, I didn't know that the first and only time I would wear this dress would be to the funeral of the one who helped pick it out.

I gathered with my and Drew's family in the "family room" at Sol Levinson & Bros., Inc. Funeral Home. I was told that guests would walk through the family room to pay respects before entering the chapel. I expected there to be a sea of people flowing through the space, though the number that did was modest at best. I became furious. Where the hell was everyone!? How dare people not show up for Drew! We all followed the last people to enter the room into the large chapel that to my amazement was completely filled with guests, not only in the pews but standing cramped in the back. There must have been hundreds of people there. The service started as I sat in the front row next to his parents and brother. Before I was called up to give the eulogy, the cantor spoke about the impact Drew had in his AA community. She then asked those who felt comfortable and were in the AA community to stand. I turned around in my seat, and to this day, what I saw is still one of the most incredible and beautiful sights that I have ever seen. At least a hundred people must have stood up. The abundance of people standing, people that Drew had affected in this wide yet family-like community, brought tears to my eyes. Unfortunately, I know that Drew did not know the impact he made on others to this extent. How important he was in so many people's lives. But at that moment, I knew he could see it. A standing ovation from the people who could understand him best.

After the service, people joined for the funeral repast at Michael's Café, Drew's job where we had first met. Drew was loved by the owner and his fellow employees there, so it was only appropriate. It was lovely to see again how many people Drew had impacted. Though the restaurant was packed, I felt lonely in the sea of people. What was I doing here without Drew? It was as if I was expecting him to come up by my side at any moment. There was a slideshow of pictures that a family friend put together playing above the bar. Friends of Drew's whom I had never met were coming up to me, introducing themselves and saying beautiful words. Drew's mother told me later that she had multiple people come up to her, stating that if it hadn't been for Drew being who he was, a helper and giver in the recovery community, that their child would be dead. This has been bound with me as a testament to who I knew him to be.

The repast was also when I was introduced to Drew's ex-girlfriend, Emily. As I stood there, statue-like with my flattened affect, she came up to me crying and gave me a hug. Anger was ignited in me. Drew and others had told me about this "toxic" relationship. Drew even casually brought this up again in conversation one week before he died. Even with his grim description of the relationship, I stood up for her and tried to give her the benefit of the doubt in what we were talking about. Though now with her arms wrapped around me and feeling her tears on my neck, I had no will to stand up for anyone. All I thought about was how maddening it was to see her grieve the way she was when I knew how she treated him. How sick it was that I felt like I needed to console *her* as she outwardly showed emotional grief. And most of all, how fucked I felt it was that she saw us as equals, that we *both* lost a boyfriend.

What I had found disrespectful soon turned threatening in my mind, which exposed my rage. My urge to make sure she knew her place and that *my grief* was greater and more valid. I was fiercely protective of my grief. I thought that she did not get to grieve in the same way that I did; she lost that privilege when she broke up with Drew. I felt like I had to advocate for Drew since he wasn't here to do it himself. I held onto this anger for a long time, even though I tried to get rid of it. I didn't want it. But it took years to let it all go and to recognize I was displacing my anger due to my complicated grief. I remember to validate myself for how I felt the day of the repast and how I felt towards her for far too long after. My feelings are valid. My grief is valid. But holding on to the anger I had towards her didn't wind up serving any purpose in the end.

Wednesday, August 12, 2015

8:18 p.m.

Dear Drew,

I'm a little pissed and hurt right now. I just went on your Facebook page, and I saw that Tyler, Hannah, and Emily posted about the recovery house that Jack, and I guess Tyler ... started in your name. I think that this is so amazing, and I feel petty and childish thinking this, but I'm fucking pissed that Tyler didn't tell me. I'm not surprised since he hasn't returned my texts in months, and I think that is real fucked up, and I know you would too. What I think I am actually angry about, though, is not the fact that Tyler and Hannah posted about this, but Emily did. I have this internal turmoil with her that I can't shake. It doesn't keep me up at night (I have other things), but it pisses me off. I know this sounds dumb, and you would tell me that I'm being ridiculous, but I feel like she doesn't have the right to be grieving like she is. There. She came up to me the day of the funeral because she wanted to meet me ... and she was a wreck, understandably. But I was trying to be human and make her feel better when all I could think about was all of the terrible things you said about her. I remember when we first started dating, I wanted to know about her. Not like in a weird or obsessive kind of way, but I wanted to know what she was like because you said you loved her, so getting to know who she was and who she was to you was being closer and more intimate with you as a person and as a partner. I liked hearing about her, but as you would bring her up on occasion, it was all very negative. Exactly a week before you died, we were at Cheesecake, and you told me that she was abusive to you. That when you were with her, you sometimes felt like you were in an abusive relationship. So, when I met her about a week and a half later, I didn't want to console her; I wanted to fucking hit her for hurting you and treating you like shit when all you did was love her and care for her. I don't like her. I never will like her. I wrote pretty much everything I just said to Hannah in a message on Facebook. I needed to get it off my chest. I was so angry. It's stupid because I shouldn't even be focused on her or who is even sharing this information. I should just be happy that the information about the recovery house is getting passed around and that Jack got it up and running. I'm very proud of him, and I know that you would feel very honored. That is what's important. I wish you were here to calm me down and tell me I'm being stupid and that she doesn't matter, and you love me. For some stupid reason, I need to know that you love me and not her when I know that this is a fact. I just miss you, and I need you here. I need validation when I'm not

feeling like a warrior. I need you to tell me
I am.

I love you, babe,

Arielle

To my anger,   my resentment,   my baggage

You are like snakeskin blowing in the wind of my deep exhale

Once protecting me from the ruthless exposure of the world

Once useful and now a mask that has been left behind

You are no longer needed

3

Trigger Warning

My grief felt like what I imagine drowning feels like.

The thing is, though, it's not as quick, and you have your friends and your family around you, sticking their hands out as far as they are able to … but not quite far enough to pull you out of the water.

My grief manifests to physical pain that must be real because it feels like my heart has just been ripped from my body, and then someone puts a sandbag on me, and I can't get up or move or breathe.

My grief is waking up in the middle of the night from a hell-like night terror only to remember that the hell actually starts when I open my eyes.

I scream and cry and rock myself back and forth while saying,

"You're okay, you're safe. You're okay, you're safe."

Am I?

My grief is bargaining with God,

Who I am sure at this point doesn't exist because why would She let this happen?

Saying that I would sacrifice years off my life, just so I could have ten more minutes with him.

My grief is listening to friends say things like,

"If my boyfriend died, I don't know what I would do. I think I would die too."

I laugh.

I say to them … You think that you would.

And you would welcome death.

Wish it, even.

But no.

Instead, you will sit in this grief that is so consuming you're actually amazed it doesn't kill you.

And for those of us lucky enough, you survive.

Some days with your head barely above water.

But eventually, you find the bottom and kick yourself back up.

And swim for your fucking life.

Saturday, August 1, 2015

12:48 a.m.

Dear Drew,

So, I just finished watching some of *Wet Hot American Summer*. It's on Netflix, so if you were here, I feel like we would be watching it together. Anyway, there is this kid on there. He is one of the campers, and his name is Drew. And I feel like you and him are really, really similar. In a way, he kind of looks like you, he just has red hair, but looking at a picture of you when you were little and looking at him, I see a resemblance. Anyway, the stuff he says is so absurd and weird and funny that he reminds me of you. I think if you were watching it, you would think so too. He is kind of an asshole, but as soon as I heard his name was Drew, I liked him. Today, Denise gave me this painting she did. It's a picture of us at the beach. The last picture we took together also happens to be one of my favorites. But it is so good. I started crying when I saw it, and the letter she wrote with it is really amazing. She said it was unfinished, like your relationship, and our plans, and our time together. Everything she wrote was so perfect. I wish I could show you it. You are still the first person I want to tell or talk to or show something to when something happens. Then, if that thing is about you, it's a bigger reminder that I can't. Kind of takes my breath away or makes the hole in my chest come back. I miss you so much. I know I say this a lot, but the things I would give to have you back, babe. As I write this and think about it, the hole gets bigger; there is a bigger void than there was earlier in the day. My heart breaks again. You know what I hate? When people say they will be there for you, day or night, anytime I need them, or I want to talk, or I need anyone. Because the truth is, they aren't. People have lives and do things and sleep. Even the people that mean it when they say it and have good intentions never live up to it. It's impossible. I am including myself in this category. People aren't waiting for my text or call. They will respond when they are free, whether I am just saying hi, or I'm lonely, or I want to die. I just have to wait for someone. That sucks, but it's life. I'm reading a book where a boy kills himself, shoots himself. I feel like everything I read now deals with grief or death or something like that. Maybe I'm looking to relate to something. Sure, let's go with that. Anyway, in the book, the boy writes a note to his mom and leaves it. It says, "Sorry, Mom, but I was below empty."[1] That has really stuck with me. Although I know this was an accident, I wonder if you felt "below empty," which is maybe why you were using. I don't know, though, because

---

[1] Hand, *The Last Time We Say Goodbye.*

when we spoke that week, you seemed okay. We just made up, we were great, we had sex again, but you weren't okay. I'm so sorry I didn't see that. I'm sorry you didn't let me see that. It's hard to live with that some days, babe. Sometimes, I feel responsible, and I know you would get so angry and sad if you knew I felt this way because I know you would say the only person to blame is yourself, but that's not good enough for me. I want you here. I want you back. I want my old life back. I want our life together back. I still have trouble accepting reality some days. It's hard to live in a reality that you aren't in anymore. Show me you see me, though. Give me a sign, please.

I love you, beautiful,

Arielle

This is hard to talk about.

Following Drew's death, I very seriously considered taking my own life. Some people in my life know this; most don't. Surprisingly, it is not at the top of the list for dinner conversation topics. Looking back on 2015, months, weeks, and days run together. I feel grateful for the part of me that wanted to start writing letters to Drew because it turned out to be descriptive documentation of who I was that year. It was the evidence of my truth when I think my memory is untrustworthy or skewed. Grief tends to be a tricky bitch like that. From my memory of that time, as well as reading the letters, I was thinking about suicide more than I wasn't.

It must have been around three or four o'clock in the morning. I have a selective memory of the year that changed everything. There are some things that I can remember down to the last detail and others that I feel like I wasn't even there to bear witness to. In any case, it was very late, or very early, depending on perspective, and the painkillers in my mother's bedroom next to mine were sounding pretty appetizing. So appetizing, I was thinking about eating all of them. I wish I could identify what it was about *that* night that made it worse than the others. That is the night when action and I sat at the same table, and it dared me to take it. Over the years, when I have reflected on this, I don't really know what it was exactly that stopped me from taking action that night. Evidently, though, something did. In a time where nothing made sense in my grief-filled life, not acting on my suicidal impulse was one of the only things that did. Maybe it was the fact that so many tears were coming down from my eyes that I couldn't see in front of me to get up from my bed to go look for these painkillers. Maybe it was because I was supposed to start a nannying job that Monday, and I couldn't let those parents down, you know, with being dead and all. I was actively thinking about killing myself, and my responsibilities to strangers battled it out to be the star of the show. Maybe it was the fact that I have *"Born to be brave, born to survive, 10.14.90-3.6.15"* tattooed on me. Having those words signify such importance to me, only then to take my own life, would be an irony that even my afterlife self could barely live with. Not to mention, I was also supposed to get lunch with a friend that week. I simply just did not have the time to kill myself. How ridiculous. There was too much to do.

Six years later, I think I figured it out. It was the "what if": what if it's the wrong decision; what if it doesn't work; what if I fuck myself up even more than I am now; what if my death leads to more death, as Drew's would have if I did this; what if it doesn't take away the pain—it just gives it to someone else? The foundational feeling I recognized in this was straight-up fear. Now *that's* what I call a protective factor.

Baruch Hashem.

I had the good sense to know that this was a "too close for comfort" encounter, and for my own safety, I needed to tell someone. The person I told was a best friend of more than ten years. Three weeks after I shared this with her, she told me that she did not think we should be friends anymore. And the stabs keep comin'.

It took years for me to forgive and understand the hurt of losing her, additionally brought into my life in a bonus round of grief. I am now able to hold compassion for my twenty-four-year-old self who was terrified, vulnerable, and just trying to do the safe thing. I also hold compassion for my friend who also must have been scared and lost as to how to handle this responsibility I put on her. It must have been hard to watch me grieve in such a way that would eventually risk my safety. I would like to think that since we had been friends for so long and because of what she did for a living, she was the person who I could go to. It didn't go to plan. I miss her. I think about her often. Grief brings out the best, worst, and truest version of people. Some of it hurts, and it hurts really bad. Some of it is surprising and gets you through the days that feel unbearable. And some of it is beautiful because you realize you are not alone in this place that will show you every shade of color, light, and darkness— and I suggest you let it.

Sunday, July 19, 2015

1:24 a.m.

Dear Drew,

When I woke up this morning, the sheets didn't
smell like you anymore. I don't know why. Part
of me thinks it's because I slept in them, but
another part of me thinks that you made them
smell like you just for last night because I
needed you here. I felt really depressed
today. Talking to people makes me want to cry.
I don't want to be around people or do
anything. I feel like this feeling won't end,
and I don't know what to do. Thabita texted me
asking if she could come over, and I said no.
She came anyway and lay silently in bed with
me as I cried for an hour. That is a good
friend. I really love her. I wanted to tell
her how I have been feeling and how I'm really
not okay. I wanted to tell her that I think
about killing myself. I don't know if I wanted
to tell her because it was true or because I
just need people to know how bad it is
sometimes. But the truth is I don't want to
die. It scares the shit out of me that I think
of doing that. I didn't want her to freak out
or get scared, even though maybe a part of me
did so other people would know how serious it
is, but I eventually told her that I think
about dying all the time, but I don't want to

die. She took me driving for over an hour, got me Starbucks and Chinese food, and we ended up back at her house hanging out. I had a nice time. I ended up telling her I have to make a conscious decision every day not to kill myself. Sometimes, I find this kind of true, and other days, I find it extremely true. I do want to take painkillers, though. I want to be numb. I wish I had morphine, but I feel like if I did, I wouldn't be able to stop, and that scares me. I feel like there are bugs crawling all over me. I don't sleep anymore; it's all fucked up. I want Dad to move to Canada. I wish you were here, baby. I want to hear your voice. I want to hear you say you love me, and everything is going to be amazing, even if it's not. I don't feel loved, and I miss feeling love. I only want to be loved by you. I feel very destructive, but at the same time, I don't want to mess up my life. A part of me wants someone to find this. A part of me wants to go to a hospital and tell them I want to kill myself. I don't want my life to get fucked up, and I don't want to not go to school or not be able to go to New Zealand because of a suicide attempt or threat. I don't know how to handle this. I don't know what the right thing is to do. I almost feel like I don't have "time for suicide." That is the stupidest shit I have ever heard. What the fuck is wrong with me? Maybe that's a sign that I don't want to do it. I don't know. I feel like no one in my life can handle my life right now, which is maybe the reason why I feel like people are dropping off. I don't know anyone who could handle me telling them I want to kill myself. Maybe I should tell my therapist. She is the only one that could "handle it," but I'm afraid of what she will do. I don't want to go to a psych hospital. I'm not sick like that. I just need help. I want help on my own terms, which I don't think exists. It took a lot to say something to Thab today. I can't imagine saying it again to someone. It's too much pressure. Maybe I'll read this to my therapist. What's fucked up is that I know how I would kill myself. I would overdose on painkillers. I feel like I would do that because that's passive and stereotypical for a female to do because there is a chance that I wouldn't die. I could still get help. But then I would be fucked for life after. I just want people to know I need help. I feel too fucking smart to kill myself, yet I think about it all the time. I want to feel loved, and I want you back. I really wish I could talk to you. I love you and miss you, and I wish you would come back to me.

I love you,

Arielle

Pain is an innate part of the human experience

Sometimes you just have to be sad as shit for a little bit

Tuesday, July 21, 2015

12:47 a.m.

Dear Drew,

I realize that I always write these very late,
technically on the following day than what I
had just had. I started that babysitting job.
It was easy, and the kids were cute. I think
it will be a good distraction during the day.
I told Cora that I was feeling suicidal. She
went behind my back and told my mom when I
asked her not to. I feel like I am in a prison
now. There wasn't a big intervention like I
was expecting, but my mom talked to me. It was
alright until the end, when I had the courage
to bring up her saying that I should be put on
medication right after I told her you died.
Fuck, that hurts. I felt that. She denied it,
saying we have "very different memories of
that day." Because there is never any way she
could be wrong or apologize for something that
felt like a stab to the chest. What this was
saying to me is that my memory was wrong; I
was mistaken; I made it up. The "I'm sorry YOU
feel that way" thing. She didn't even think
maybe it was her that was mistaken. I have
replayed that day a thousand times over in my
head; I know what happened. Her denying it
happened may have hurt worse. Oh, and then she
took medication from my room. 2007 all over

again. I am angry with Cora, but I don't blame her. I would have done the exact same thing, if not worse. I know the drill. That feeling of forgetting that you are really gone and then remembering it happened today. Like a hammer in the chest. Your pictures still look and feel so real. Those were moments in time captured forever. I remember how I felt in those moments, and knowing that I won't have them again is actually unbelievable and incredibly painful. I'll talk to Cora in a couple of days. I need to get my shit together. I'll try and go to the gym this week. And I will try and stay positive. I can only imagine what kind of bullshit this week will reel in. My old bus driver posted a picture of me in middle school getting on the bus. It's horrific. My first instinct was to tell you about it and show you so I could hear you laugh really hard and make fun of me. I loved showing you old pictures. I miss the ever-loving shit out of you. Oh, and I listen to country music now. I'm sure you can't believe it. Randy Houser came on the radio, "Runnin' Outta Moonlight." It made me cry because I could just picture you in your car singing it to me. We never had a song. Maybe that can be it.

Love and miss you more than ever,

Arielle

There is a common misbelief that talking about suicide or asking if someone is suicidal will "plant" the idea of suicide or increase suicidal ideation. However, what the research about suicidal ideation has shown, that can be seen in dozens of published findings, is that there is no evidence to this. In fact, it is quite on the contrary. In a review of the literature in 2014 at Cambridge University, it was found that acknowledging and talking about suicide may actually decrease suicidal ideation across children and adults and may lead to improvements in mental health for treatment-seeking populations.[2]

I am reminded of this with a client I'm working with. When Keegan* was sixteen years old, he was told by his parents that he didn't need therapy; there was nothing for him to go for. Unfortunately, at the time, therapy would have been paramount for a kid who just wanted to feel safe and to be understood. Instead, at the delicate age of sixteen, Keegan began to fill his "water tank" with discomfort, hurt, anger, and pain. Only into his thirties did that water tank even come into his awareness. When Keegan first started therapy a year and a half ago, he shares how little holes started to be poked in this water tank, but as he had known and done all his life, Keegan was able to cover the holes with duct tape. Using all his energy to keep the facade that everything is fine, still able to keep the walls of the tank sturdy, and not let anyone *really* in. Not wanting to show feelings, trust, or vulnerability because he was afraid of judgment or it being used against him. Then he met me.

He and I have been working together for over a year, and he has made significant strides in the therapeutic space. Yet, progress isn't linear, and Keegan has been feeling a remarkable heaviness in his life. Today, as he reflects on a session of ours earlier in the week, he tells me this:

> You poked a hole in the water tank. Somehow, you just knew I was at a level I wasn't before, even though I was trying to pull the wool over your head. So, when you asked me if I wanted to die, I thought, I'm clearly not hiding. Part of me needs to know

---

[2] Dazzi et al., "Does asking about suicide and related behaviours induce suicidal ideation?," 3361-3363.

what I did so I can make sure not to do that again and keep the wool over people's head, and another part of me needs to know because you obviously saw something in me that I didn't.

He told me that he himself wasn't aware of how low he was feeling until that conversation. In the past, when someone, therapist or otherwise, poked holes in the tank, they were kept small, and Keegan managed to cover then in time to continue the facade.

With sarcasm and humor, he said, "Then you come along with a fucking shotgun and blow a gash in the tank, and I can't tape it back up. I don't have enough tape."

This makes me laugh pretty hard, and it make me feel good to know that even when Keegan is at one of his lowest points, both of us can still rely on the rapport that has been diligently built over time. "Yeah," I reply, "I guess you're all out."

I wish someone would have asked me. If I am being honest, I don't know if I would have answered honestly at first. But what this would have done is given me a place to go when I was thinking about it. It would have given me a person that I knew was safe and "could handle it," as this was a concern of mine when I went through the list of people in my head of who to tell after the night that was difficult to survive. I think a compelling reason why people generally don't ask about suicidal ideation is because they don't know what to do with an affirmative answer. It's a heavy weight and responsibility. Furthermore, you might be thinking, *how would I even ask?* For that, I have some answers. Through working in the mental health field in a variety of settings and a myriad of populations, I have learned that in a clinical setting, it is best to ask about suicidal ideation in at least two different ways. That said, if you aren't a medical or mental health professional, here are some options:

"I know you have been going through a really tough time, and I want to check in and ask if you ever think about hurting yourself or ending your life."

"Do you ever have thoughts of suicide?"

"I see how much pain you are in. I want you to know that I am a safe person to talk to if you have thoughts about suicide."

"I want you to know I care about you and your life, so I want to ask you, do you have thoughts about killing yourself?"

"I love you, which is why I want to ask if you ever have thoughts about hurting yourself or taking your own life."

"Do you ever feel like life isn't worth living?"

"Have you ever gone to sleep and hoped that you didn't wake up in the morning?"

My mind is evoked by a statement that was told to me years ago: *If they have the courage to ask, I have the courage to say yes.* I think of this as a reminder when talking about suicide because the statement reminds us that both parties are offering and showing vulnerability, trust, and courage. Asking someone if they are thinking about hurting themselves or ending their own life takes guts. Being on the other side of that question and giving an honest answer also takes copious amounts of strength. That's how I was able to find compassion in experiencing my friend's rejection. I know the strength it took me to tell her what I was feeling, and I would like to think she had courage in telling my mom, as she knew she couldn't hold it on her own. She did what I often tell my clients to do: find and use your resources. I did it. She did it. That's a good start.

Though this was a time of added grief, in a paradoxical way, it was also a time of resiliency and growth. My friend Cora's rejection and abrupt dismissal of our relationship, on top of the unfathomable tragedy of Drew's untimely death, made me feel like I was in the deepest hole I could have imagined. Over the months that passed, it was as if I went back and forth between adding scoops of dirt to fill the void and, just as quickly, letting it sink me deeper and deeper as I shovel the dirt out again. The incident of a betrayal from my best friend turned out to be a catalyst in an ascending direction; when there's no more dirt to dig, there's only one way to go. I made the conscious choice to not let this destroy my life, as I have seen it done to others. It was time to stand up at the bottom of the hole, find a rope, and pull myself up. Sometimes, I had people helping me, and other times, I strictly only had my upper body strength, which, let's face it, is a work in progress in itself. Somehow, though, I did it, I do it, and I will keep doing it because grief is not linear. It is often closer in relation to a two-year-old's art project on a dining room wall than any logical graph.

It is strange to write about this and remember it when I know what my life looks like now. This wasn't a defining moment for me, and it's still hard to think that I was ever this low. In the words of Derek DelGaudios, "I am not just defined by what you see. I am also defined by all the things you will never see. We all are."[3]

---

[3] DelGaudio, *In & Of Itself.*

I do it for you

The brave girl who defies complacency

The one who isn't afraid to fly

Baptized by the angry skies

To soar across the sea in the hands of technology

And the one who finally picked up the phone

I'm still here. For you.

To the ones dancing loud and singing hard

To the tears that blind your eyes

That pierce your skin

The lashes that get lost

And the person who keeps moving anyway

I do it for you.

To my friend who said nothing

Just sitting there being

I'm still here. For you.

And for the friend who thought too much

For the friend who edited the past

The friend who left me for dead

Fuck you.

I do it for you

To show you I can

To show them how it's done

A hard fight I thought I won

4

This is Chaos

W e are the experiences we have and the response to challenges
that are presented to us. We are made up of the traumas that
we survive and the resilience we find. We are who we love and
who we let love us. We are the lessons, the heartbreaks, and the
celebrations. We are what we believe in. We are as much of what we fail
in as our biggest successes. We are the stories that were told to us and the
stories that we will tell others. And still, unreliable narrators of each
other's life stories. We are complex and multilayered beings.

2015 was the most dialectical year of my life. Not only did I
feel an assemblage of emotions, but I would feel seemingly opposite
emotions at the same time. I was exhausted, confused, and self-
critical. Was I completely unhinged or just in grief? For me, they
were one in the same. I remember telling one of my friends, "Grief
does weird things to you, man … " in a *Dazed and Confused* kind
of way, with less drugs and more confusion.

In my current therapy practice, I often use dialectical
behavior therapy, or DBT. It's a form of cognitive behavioral
therapy, or CBT, that focuses on regulating one's emotions and
improving relationships.[1] No matter who my client is and why they
are seeking therapy, I find DBT to be an incredibly helpful model
because it's skill based. In the mental health world, we often hear

---

[1] Pederson and Pederson, *The Expanded Dialectical Behavioral Therapy Skills Training Manual*, 1–8.

that a good therapist will start talking about termination in the first session. I may see the use of DBT skills to determine a timeline for termination of therapy, as well as remind clients that these skills are added to their toolbox of coping skills for an array of different emotionally or interpersonally challenging predicaments. It's quite the bummer to now know how helpful this could have been for me at the time of my debilitating grief. But alas, I found other ways to cope.

I could see it in your eyes

You wanted to say something

Maybe that you will miss me

Maybe that you love me

I saw it there, in your eyes

Speaking more than your lips ever could

But we stayed silent

You wishing things were different

Me wanting to hear, "I love you"

Because I guess I miss hearing it from someone

Even though I knew I couldn't say it back

So, we stayed silent

And listened to the rain

Saturday, September 5, 2015

12:40 a.m.

Dear Drew,

Fuck, tonight was terrible. I feel like a horrible person. I just really feel like shit about myself and everything. I had class today. The first day of class and I didn't go. I forgot. And I just remembered about ten minutes ago. I don't know what is wrong with me. Something is fucking wrong. Oh, you died. That's what is fucking wrong with me. It is fucking me up because now, every semi-exciting thing like going out with a guy that I used to date but I am not even fucking interested in and he has a girlfriend takes up most of my brain space, enough that I fucking forget I have school. I feel fucked up. I want to cry. I want you. I'm drunk. Why the fuck am I drunk? Why did I drink? Now I feel even worse. And I start the new job tomorrow. Fuck, I hate everything. I am not in the right frame of mind, but I need money. Having a job isn't convenient. How the fuck am I supposed to know when I will be triggered or when the depression comes back? Fuck. I am sad as fuck right now. If you were here, everything would be better and fine and would be happy, and you could be happy. I fucking miss you so much, and I hate you for leaving me. Everyone is happy but me. And I know that's not even true, but it's not fucking fair. I have to be in so much pain all of the time, every second of the day. And other people can be happy. Other people can be in love. I have to be in pain because you decided to stick a fucking needle in your arm like a fucking idiot. Fuck you. Fuck you for doing that to me and for doing that to yourself and your friends and your parents. You fucking piece of shit. I fucking have no one now. No one to love me because you fucking died.

You break my heart how much I need you and love you,

Arielle

I stare into the mirror while the flood of tears moisturizes my skin

This is one of my rawest forms

My lips cracked from my mouth open wide, trying to catch my breath while I let the pain escape me

My back is hunched over because something is pulling my heart from my chest

How can a sandcastle feel like it's on top of me, holding me down?

And I'm screaming

Screaming out while my heart feels like it is being forcefully separated from my body—

Do you feel your hand is on the other end?

This body that you loved

Now missing the part that loves you

> *So   fucking   in   love   with   you*

My mind is questioning why we did this, why we let it get this far, knowing it would hurt this much

My vision is blurred with tears when I remember your face or what it felt like that first night together

This is what it has come to

And you don't even know

This is what it looks like when my heart breaks

Monday, August 24, 2015

10:52 p.m.

Dear Drew,

I just got this powerful feeling of missing you. Intensely. Thinking about it, staying in the emotion and feeling, brings tears to my eyes. I fucking miss you so much. So, so, so much. I didn't think it was possible. I didn't think you dying was possible. You know, I obviously wish you were here. I never thought this would be the end of your life and the beginning of a new life for me without you, something I never wanted to do. But knowing what I know now, just how miserable you were, truly, I am so sorry you lived that way. I am sorry I didn't know. I am sorry you felt like you needed to fix it on your own. I'm sorry the only way you thought you could get through was heroin. I am so fucking sorry, baby. I'm so sorry. I cry as I write this. You would tell me not to worry because everything will be amazing. I'm trying to make it amazing. But it is hard to do that without you. But I want to do it for you, for both of us. That big life I am always talking about, I am trying to make it amazing. I just wish I didn't have to live it for you. I don't want to be strong, and I don't want to be brave. I want to fall apart in your arms, soaking your shirt with my tears and spit. And you do not say anything about it because you know I have to get it out. You just hold me. Maybe you would say, "no, no, no" when I start crying, but then you just let me go, full force. It doesn't matter how much pain I am feeling or if I am scared because at least I am in your arms. I am safe. I am with you, and you are with me. And you love me. I want to feel your arms, your warmth. I want that back in my life. But I know you aren't coming back. Just in my dreams, maybe. I think you were in my dream last night. I can't remember what it was about. I feel like it was sexual, though I don't know. I just know it has been the third time you have been in my dreams since you have died. Yup, stab. I'm going to wrap myself in the comforter and your blanket of shirts. Pretend you are next to me. Please be with me.

I unconditionally love you always,

Arielle

One of the best skills in DBT that I have found not only helpful for clients but helpful to myself as well is "Walking the Middle Path." This is a core concept in DBT because it puts dialectical thinking within the language we use: *I can feel heartbroken about my loss, AND I can still laugh when something is funny.*[2] Accepting and understanding this way of thinking is so unfamiliar to most. I've been told on more than a few occasions from clients that it's a "mindfuck." When we use the word "and" rather than "but," it validates both sides of the sentence and reminds us that not only is it possible, but it's common to feel two different things at once. It can be a tough skill and concept because it challenges narratives that many of us have held throughout our lives and says, *forget that—now think like this and soak in the self-validation!*

The middle path is a great tool to battle the guilt that so often rides shotgun with grief. I felt so much pain from this loss every day and would say that I would do anything to be relieved from feeling like that. And at the same time, when I wasn't outwardly grieving and feeling the intensity of the pain, I felt so guilty. I created narratives that I now know were arbitrary and simply untrue: if I don't feel pain, I don't miss him; people will think I'm over it if I allow myself to have fun; if I don't connect to the pain of grief, then I can't connect to my creativity; if I'm not thinking about him every second, that means I don't love him. The truth is that I will miss, love, and grieve the loss of Drew until the day I die, and how that shows up for me will change throughout the days, months, and years. That's okay. I can be reminded of Drew and not break down in devastation and pulsating pain. I can say that I don't always feel him with me, and I know that doesn't demean my connection to him. I feel immense gratitude for the life I have created for myself, and I still hold a strong desire and sadness that I am not living the life I had imagined with Drew. Understanding that I don't always have control over my emotions or when they will arrive and depart has been hard to accept. Though, learning to accept it has given me the gift of self-compassion in my grief, which has been the most

---

[2] Pederson and Pederson, *The Expanded Dialectical Behavioral Therapy Skills Training Manual,* 14–15.

influential tool I have learned. Accompanying the middle path, self-compassion has been the ammunition strong enough to fight guilt.

My reaction to Drew's death and the secondary losses associated with it ranged from complete physical, mental, and emotional debilitation to what I would describe as a manic gratitude. The way my grief showed up felt chaotic, to say the least. Something that I've noticed as I go back and read the letters I wrote to Drew was the intense change in emotion or mood. Quite honestly, it made me feel like I was on the verge of a psychotic break sometimes. Just how furious I could feel, followed by insurmountable amounts of sadness. And then the next day, being able to have a nice day with a friend, and by the time I was writing the letter to Drew that night, telling him about my fun day, the wave of grief would hit, and I could feel like life wasn't worth living. The anger sticks out in my mind. It was vicious. Anger towards Drew, the world, other people, and myself.

Saturday, September 5, 2015

11:55 p.m.

Dear Drew,

I wanted to start this letter off with it still being the 5th. Tomorrow is six months. But today, six months ago, you were alive. You were telling me you loved me. You were making me laugh. That makes me happy and sad to think about. But I want to spend the last five minutes of today thinking about that and how special today was six months ago, and I didn't even know it. I wish I did, babe; I would have done anything to get to you. To be with you. To hold you. To save you. I love you, completely, fully, wholeheartedly, and unconditionally. I am going to do something for myself tomorrow and something for you. I am going to do yoga with some friends in the morning, and then I am going to the cemetery. I think I am going to bring my computer, maybe a book, and hang out with you. Think about you, miss you, love you. It is now midnight. You left me six months ago. You may have been gone before that; I will never know. All I know is that I miss you every day. I still feel you and your love and your presence. I feel and see the signs you give me to let me know you are here. They are not going unnoticed. I wrote about you tonight. And I submitted it. I hope it gets published. I am proud of it. I am proud of it because it is about you. You would be proud of it too. I hope you know I am writing about you. I miss your touch. I miss your voice. I miss hearing you love me, and even if I can't hear it now, I still feel it. Thank you for loving me, baby.

I love you too,

Arielle

Sunday, September 6, 2015

10:01 p.m.

Dear Drew,

It is six months ago today that you died. I
want to die. I feel like a completely fucked-
up person. I am a storm that has run through
my friends. Tonight, I have thought about
killing myself. I have thought about cutting
myself. I will do neither. I want to go to
sleep and not wake up for days. I don't want
to be inside my own head. I want something to
put me out of this pain. I want morphine. I
want a painkiller that will stop making me
think my own thoughts. I understand why you
used. Actually, I don't, but I think I
understand part of the reason. If you were
feeling at all how I am feeling now, and then
you add the addictive behavior and history, I
don't know why I wouldn't go for drugs too. I
have the decency to think about the people I
am leaving behind, though. Maybe you didn't
think, or maybe you couldn't. I don't want to
go to school. I don't want to go to my job. I
don't want to do anything. The only thing that
is worse than doing all of that is probably
not doing all of that. Maybe I should go on
antidepressants. I don't know. I hate today.
I hate what you did to me. This isn't fucking
fair. You gave me all of your pain, and you

didn't deserve it, but I sure as fuck don't, either. I just want you back. I want the way things used to be and the way things should have been. I'm not the same person that I was in the pictures I look at. Those people don't exist anymore.

I love you,

Arielle

I tell myself it's alright as I gasp for air and clear my fogged-up eyes. Repeat it enough—pretending I can trick myself. Saying I don't need you when we both know the truth.

Monday, September 7, 2015

10:56 p.m.

Dear Drew,

Why am I even writing every night? You aren't reading these. I would like to think you are, or you can, but you can't. Maybe I am doing it to help myself. Maybe. But does it really? Am I ever going to reread these? Maybe I am just doing this so someone else can read it. So someone else can be like, "Ohhh, that's how she was feeling," or "Yeah, I felt the same way." Fuck that. To say I am writing this so other people can read it. In hopes of what, making this shit into a book? Get it published? Fuck that. Fuck you. Fuck everyone. The only person that has made me feel even a little better is Amanda. She is telling me the things I need to hear, true things that my mind won't let me think or accept right now because it is too concerned with trying to go numb. I want to be numb. I don't want to do any of this shit. I want to quit everything. I am afraid that if I do, though, then I will never get out of this stage, this funk. So, I am going to force myself to go to school and go to work. I won't want to. Maybe I'll medicate myself to do it. See how that changes my personality. My mind. Because I can't do it on my own. I can't be with my normal mind, so

I want to change it. Alter it. I don't feel loved. And when people try to love me and show me love, I push them away. I don't accept it, then get mad and sad because I feel like I don't have it. I am so fucked up. I am going to call my psychiatrist in the morning and get on medication. I can't keep living this way. I feel like I have hit rock bottom again. I was afraid this would happen at this point. I feel like a fucking prisoner in my own mind and body, and I want out. I want to get the fuck out of here.

I fucking need you,

Arielle

Another dialectical grief reaction was the experience of going to the cemetery. Though most of Drew's ashes were spread at the Grand Canyon, his family also buried some in the temple's cemetery. Before going for the first time, I thought about my grandmother, who passed away when I was eight years old. On the anniversary of her death, my mom took me to the cemetery to visit the gravesite. I was expecting to be beside myself in grief when we got there, but I didn't feel anything. It was probably one of the first times that I had experienced conflicting and confusing feelings in grief. Losing my grandma made a significant dent in my life, even at eight years old, and it was extremely hard for me to take on and accept. So having little to no reaction was strange for me. What is so vivid about this memory, however, is walking back into my grandpa's house in Fall River, Massachusetts, and almost instantly feeling her presence that overpowered me with grief. It was a full-body experience so robust that left me both in such sorrow and familiar, embracing love. Comforted by my family, I talked to my mom about the differences in the experiences. Through exploring this, we concluded that sure, my grandmother's body was at the cemetery, but her soul and everything she was were still at home with us. It was *her* love that rushed me as I walked in the house, too big to be contained in a box four feet underground.

This on my mind, wondering if I would "feel anything" at the cemetery, scared the shit out of me. Again, even with this memory of my grandma, I still played with arbitrary truths. First fearing that I was going to lose it and cause a scene, then thinking of the pain I would feel and what it would mean if I felt nothing. Trapping myself in a never-winning cycle of "If I feel Drew here, then he will never be with me anywhere else, but if I don't feel him here, then something is wrong with me, and he isn't with me." That first time was with his family, following a service held on the property. We walked over together, looking for the temporary white "name tag" staked in the ground while we waited for the headstone to be made. We placed stones around his name and recited the *El Malei Rachamim* prayer, partaking in the mitzvah of commemorating the burial and the life.

I felt removed, not fully present. Maybe I was back in some form of denial or protection, but it didn't feel comfortable to be vulnerable around so many people. I suppressed most of what I was feeling, which didn't feel like much. I felt uncomfortable in my own skin. Was I experiencing something like when I was eight years old, standing at the grave of my grandmother? I came back to Drew's grave more times than I could count. I went weekly for a while, then more randomly, fighting off the judgmental self-talk I had in my head about the change in frequency. I would always feel differently when I would go. Often feeling so sad but not being able to grieve fully in the way I wanted to at the grave. Sometimes sitting on a blanket to read or write, I would often find myself in a state of creativity among the dead. Always talking to Drew to some length and either turning on music that fit my temperament that day or finding peace in the sound of the deceased. There were days where I would show up, and I felt Drew so fiercely, it was like he welcomed me to my reserved seat next to him. Dissimilarly, every so often, I would pull up, sit on the ground, and feel completely, bitterly isolated. What I could habitually count on, however, was the sun. She would always come out, even just for a couple of moments, reminding me I wasn't alone.

Dissociating from the limited view of a life. A gold plate and stone with a name and a date now represent an entire human being and soul. There's no way to wrap your head around that connection. But I do think it's a nice way to honor Drew, to be with his body, the physical representation that was shown to the world of who he was. There's a disconnection, though, and it feels like just a name on stone in the ground.

The grass is extra sharp here

I run my fingers through it, hesitating because I don't want to cut myself on the unexpected yet familiar roughness when my skin changes direction

The unkept overlap over the golden plate reminds me of forgotten souls

I run my fingers through it like I forgot what it felt like

I sit on the wet ground trying to ignore the ants that I implicitly feel exploring my clothes

I sit among the ripped pieces of the book left in your honor

The book that you held close to your heart

Mother Earth and Father Sky joining in the elements that turned the paper into tissue

This is the meeting place of grief and gratitude

Of creativity and dismantling sorrow

The hidden pathways in my brain that were dimly lit, now coming to the forefront of my limbic system

It's the partner dance of the implicit and explicit memories that I feel come rushing in when I'm here

Now thinking that the grass lying wild on the golden plate and stone is the perfect representation of how it was

You and I, wild for each other, going smoothly in one direction

Then it cuts me

And I realize that what seemed whole can now be torn apart, string by string

And I felt the roughness all the way down

5

It Starts Somewhere

Cleaning out the space of a loved one that is no longer here is a Herculean effort. It goes against all these rules you have come up with in your head that make it seem like there are still things you can control about an uncontrollable situation. I met Drew's parents at his house in Baltimore to clean out his room a couple of weeks after the funeral. The energy was a mixture of emotional struggle and checking something off a to-do list. I took a large pile of T-shirts, a composition book, an almost-empty Carmex lip balm, a hairbrush, his Alcoholics Anonymous blue book and sobriety medallions, two books that I gave him, a Ninja Turtle onesie that I got for him, and a bed comforter that had not yet been opened because we were waiting to use it for when we moved in together. The bed comforter was a birthday gift he gave to me ... for his own bed ... cheekily calling it "our bed" to rectify the purchase when he asked, "Did I fuck up?"

I still have all of these items, except for the Carmex. I kept this for years, and it was an extremely difficult decision to dispose of the now-empty tube. This was something that Drew had touched, not only with his hands but with his lips. Putting my lips to it, feeling the smooth surface before the balm moisturized my lips in the same way it did his. This felt like a piece of him. I kept even the empty tube for at least a year. Until one day, I was strong enough to let this small piece of Drew go, logically knowing though still trying to believe that it would be okay with him to do so. The T-shirts were cut up and made into a blanket by my friend Tori. A gift that is still so special, I sleep with it nightly, even now. The heaviness of it feels like his arm around me when our bodies would be spooned into each other, a tactile memory that crosses my mind often.

I still have most of the sobriety medallions, though some of them are no longer in my possession. I sent a one-year sober medallion to Tyler along with a letter. Tyler told me later that when he received the envelope, only the letter was inside. There was a tear in the corner where the medallion must have broken free in the hustle and bustle of the USPS. We both like to think that Drew had it land in someone's hands that must have needed it. There are three other medallions that are now placed around the world: Simi Valley, California; Queenstown, New Zealand; and Ko Lanta, Thailand. These are the places I traveled to after Drew's death that significantly helped me heal in my grief journey. Now, a piece of Drew will also always be there.

Tuesday, July 21, 2015

11:42 p.m.

Dear Drew,

Today was alright. Not great but better than the days prior. I met with the disability support services woman at school and got my accommodations. I really want to do my best this semester and make you proud. I think you would have been really proud of me last semester. It's weird; I got a 4.0. That has never happened before. I should be ecstatic. Even more so, I want to say, "with everything that happened," but I don't bullshit with you, and after all, you know what happened. You died. Yup, that still hurts. You died, and it crushed my world, my life, my future, me. Yet somehow, I pulled it together enough to get a 4.0. I know how proud you would be. So, I am going to try and do it again this semester. I also saw that psychologist. God, I wish I could talk to you about this guy. He is so unethical and unprofessional and a real pain in the ass to sit with for more than ten seconds. I miss shit talking with you. I ate with my mom and dad and Jadon. Jadon got his permit today; I know you would have been really excited for him. It was actually the first thing that has made me really smile in a couple of days. I also realized that people love me and care about me. I knew this, but it is easy to forget when you are feeling as low as I have been. Jen was even more upbeat today. I really like talking to her. She told me that since I don't see you in my dreams, if she sees you, she will tell you that I love you and you need to come visit me in mine. I would really like that, so come on. I felt more like a person today. Nick made me feel really good. He is a really good friend. I think you would be proud and happy about the way he treats me and how he has been showing up for me, especially when I don't have it in me to show up for myself. When I read what he wrote to me today, it brought tears to my eyes. I'm glad I have him. You would be too. I bought lipstick today because I feel better when I feel pretty, and I feel powerful when I wear lipstick. I need that power back. I think I am even going to go to the gym tomorrow. I sent Jen a picture of my tattoo, and she sent me this poem. I think it is perfect and beautiful, just like you.

"The Dash" by Linda Ellis

I read of a man who stood to speak at the funeral of a friend. He referred to the dates on the tombstone from the beginning ... to the end.

He noted that first came the date of birth and spoke the following date with tears, but he said what mattered most of all was the dash between those years.

For that dash represents all the time that they spent alive on earth. And now only those who loved them know what that little line is worth.

For it matters not, how much we own, the cars ... the house ... the cash. What matters is how we live and love and how we spend our dash.

So, think about this long and hard. Are there things you'd like to change? For you never know how much time is left that can still be rearranged.

If we could just slow down enough to consider what's true and real and always try to understand the way other people feel.

And be less quick to anger and show appreciation more and love the people in our lives like we've never loved before.

If we treat each other with respect and more often wear a smile, remembering that this special dash might only last a little while.

So, when your eulogy is being read, with your life's actions to rehash ... would you be proud of the things they say about how you spent your dash?[1]

I love and miss you terribly, babe,

Arielle

---

[1] Ellis, "Dash Poem: Live Your Dash."

About a month after Drew's death, I started to see Erin, my grief therapist. What's kind of funny about thinking back on my work with her was that I actually don't remember most of it. I don't recall any revelations that I had in that space (though I am sure I must have had some), and nothing that she said sticks out in my mind. Even with that being true, what I do remember was the space that she created for me. I remember feeling comfortable enough to win the ugly cry contest time and time again. I remember getting so angry at her a couple of times that I was either yelling and cursing or sitting there fuming in silence, and she continued to give and hold the space that I needed, knowing it wasn't personal, and I was in grief, and my emotions were constantly heightened. I remember the faces she would make and her body language when I was in uncontrollable sadness. I remember her sharing parts of her own grief that made me feel less alone in mine. She is a phenomenal therapist. She knew that nothing she could say would make it better, but being there for me every week was something I could count on and stabilize me when nothing else felt like it could.

Erin was also who introduced me to GRASP—Grief Recovery After a Substance Passing. I told her that I wanted to join a support group for those who have lost loved ones to a drug overdose. We both looked and searched our networks, as I myself was in graduate school for social work and couldn't come up with anything. Erin then told me about GRASP, which was a support network with meetings all around the country, and told me that she could see me starting a group on my own. After not much convincing, I had something I could put my energy towards that made me feel purposeful and in line with what I wanted to do after grad school. I spoke to the GRASP organization founder and organizers to help get me set up with material to market to my community in Howard County since I was now living back at home. Before I knew it, only three months after Drew's death, I started to facilitate GRASP Howard County. Though I had experience leading therapeutic groups before, this was the first time that I was both a member and a facilitator. Being in this role felt important to me, as I was now the one to create a space for others and their grief. This was one of the first ways that it felt like I honored Drew. Doing something for the community that understood me, just like he impacted his community that understood him. The turnout month-to-month was significant enough to make me feel like there was a need that was not previously being met. And I was doing something about it.

I sit on a dead and fallen tree

The yellow wedding bells in the distance do not chime as they once did

A deceased rebel, now broken all over

This was me

This tree won't come back to life, as I did

Home for moss and mushrooms now

Still producing life, even after death

That is familiar

Saturday, July 18, 2015

12:23 a.m.

Dear Drew,

I can't help but smile right now because I am
so sure that you are here with me, probably
watching me write this. I met (through
Facebook) this girl Jen who is also in the
GRASP FB page. She lost her girlfriend, and
she has been one of the few people that I have
truly connected with since you have died. She
understands everything I am feeling and feels
very similar about her girlfriend, Sam, as I
do about you. We both think that you and Sam
know each other now and today were trying to
figure out a way to help us feel better. I
asked for you to stay with me today and always,
and I really feel you right now. I just changed
my sheets and got a whiff of what smelled like
you. I stuck my face into the sheets, and it
was like you were next to me. It smelled
exactly like you. It is so amazing. I can't
wait to go to sleep and have your smell wrapped
around me, as if you were right next to me,
which I imagine you to be every night. As I
write this, I wonder if me writing this will
interfere with me having the pillow talk that
I have with you every night. I am still going
to do it. It may be a little repetitive. Also,
I was really craving some potato chips, and we
didn't have any, but when I went downstairs,
I found a small individual bag, good looks. My

phone has been showing this error that says, "tag not found," as if someone is pressing something, and the phone can't respond. What is weird also is that as soon as I started typing about it just now, it stopped, and it's been happening for a while. Also, I knocked down some bracelets that I had on my dresser, and the only one out of the three left was the one that had your name. So, I know you're here. Jen told me that she writes a letter to Sam every night. I thought that was really romantic and great, and I want to try and start writing to you, too, so I can look back and keep it. Maybe you and Sam sent Jen and I to each other for help and support, so if you did, thank you. I love you and miss you more than words. I know you are here; it's not going unnoticed.

I love you,

Arielle

I was somewhere between healing myself by helping others and feeling deeply internally wounded. I knew I had people around me who loved and cared about me. I had found purpose and a way to help others that felt personal to me and a great honor to Drew. But it never felt like enough. Though I had some days where smiles formed on my consistently red face, there was a significant hole in my being. I was in a state of survival. What was interesting was that it felt comforting at times. The ache was now familiar and safe, and veering away from this was unchartered territory. My conflicting feelings battled in my head; I was so alone in my grief, yet the loneliness was computed into thinking that there was a special and intimate connection with Drew, and I didn't want anyone else to understand because it would make it less special. I would tell people that they couldn't *imagine* what I was going through. "Whatever you think this would be like, it's nothing like that." It quite literally *is* unimaginable.

The amount of pain that comes with losing a partner is so much more than one might think. Like other losses, it comes with many secondary losses piggybacking on top of it. In secondary loss, there is a snowball effect that shows the impact of the "primary loss," therefore leading to multiple other losses. It is important to understand as well that the impact isn't necessarily secondary, but rather it is a result of the primary loss. If we can understand that secondary loss is likely to happen when experiencing grief, it can increase self-awareness and help us identify complexities in our grief. There are many aspects to grief, and when we can identify what we are grieving, we can then properly mourn.[2] I lost Drew, my partner. I also lost the future I had with him, from the apartment we were two months away from getting to the years down the road living the life we created together. I lost my children that I could so vividly see. Thinking about how a little boy would resemble him when he was young, with big ears and a big smile. We would talk about our future kids often, and he would repeatedly say how much he was looking forward to being a dad. Drew always thought he

---

[2] Williams, "Secondary Loss—One Loss Isn't Enough??!!"

would be the "fun dad," and I would be the "mean mom," to which I would reply, "Well, yes, someone has to be the adult."

This has always hit hard for me. I have wanted to be a mother for most of my life, and even as a child, I took on caretaking roles in play. I have found compelling comfort in speaking to individuals who are "channels of light" and connect to something outside of our awareness following Drew's death. I am aware that this practice in itself is seen as controversial, though in my experience, it has not only alleviated some of my pain but has proven to me there is something more after death. There have been an assortment of conversations and things I have been told by mediums that have surprised me but nothing quite like the following. I saw a medium about a month after Drew passed away. I was in desperation to be close to him again, to feel connected to him, and to find out answers. I quickly adopted the role of detective. That first reading was done by an older woman named Mariah, whom my aunt had been to multiple times in Warwick, Rhode Island. The whole experience was amazing and emotional and brought more light in my life to continue feeling my grief and not hide from it. What sticks out is when she asked about a baby. She asked if Drew had a child. I said he didn't and mentioned that one of his good friends recently became a father. She then said to me these words: "He is thinking about a baby. It's his." I told her that he and I would often talk about having children. She continued, "That's it. He is so sorry he couldn't give you a baby." Cue the waterworks.

Now moving forward about one year, close to the first anniversary of Drew's death, I returned from a speaking engagement at Towson University, and I was in a bad emotional place. Driving home, I began talking to Drew, telling him that unlike other times when I would publicly speak, I didn't feel him with me. I needed to feel him. I needed to know he was watching me and next to me, begging him to show me a sign that he was there. I walked into my house, and almost immediately, my sister, Nediva, called for me from upstairs. When I walked into her room, I realized she was on a video call doing a reading with Espirito Gato—or Jessie, as we know him as. I spoke with Jessie a couple of times before: once when I was suffering through an intense illness that resulted in a thirty-day hospital stay and once after Drew passed. I sat down next to Nediva, and Jessie first asked me if I just came into the house because "he could feel the energy change." He then told me that a "young man joined the session. Your sister says that it's your boyfriend." I started crying and seemed to only be able to nod my head. "He wants you to know that he sees you and is with you." What he said next, I still cannot explain. Verbatim: "Also, he's thinking about a baby. He's feeling really sad. He is so sorry he couldn't give you a baby."

Two different people, who don't know each other, and know very little information about me, told me the exact same words. Words that they said came from Drew. It wasn't as if I was looking for proof. But if I ever doubted if Drew is with me and finds ways to connect with me or that these two individuals have a gift of connecting to a realm that is beyond the one we are all in now, this was it. The detective in me was alive for most of the year after Drew's death. It was a big move forward in my grief when I let this part of me go. It served its purpose and was no longer needed in my life. I like to think of grief in that way. We hold on to it as long as we need to, and though it is never easy, we do have the power to let go of it.

I lost a part of myself that I had no idea connected so directly to him. Being with Drew was part of who I was, my identity. With this loss came a change in identity I was not prepared to make. A missing piece that, to me, will always stay missing. And similarly, to the feeling of a special connection to Drew that came from the loneliness, I never have wanted the empty space to be completely filled. The biggest secondary loss that I feel and that also encompasses all the others is the loss of what could have been. This momentous part of grief is unmeasurable because the possibilities go far beyond imagination. Especially when I am mindful of my life now and how different it looks from when Drew died, I often think about the deviation my path would have taken if he was still alive. This can and has been a tricky part of grief due to the endless nature of "what could have been." It has been difficult for me to explain to others the extent of my mourning around this part. I have been told by others that you can't miss something you never had. This is what makes it "disenfranchised grief," or "ambiguous loss," commonly under a larger umbrella term of "complicated grief." In disenfranchised grief, there is dictation to who is entitled to grieve and over what. This, in turn, dictates who receives support, validation, and acknowledgement. When we don't feel societal acknowledgment or validation, grief becomes disenfranchised, and the grieving process gets even more confusing and isolating because now shame and fear of judgement are along for the ride. Without sufficient support, adjustment to life after a significant loss becomes even more difficult.[3] I find that giving myself a boundary of time to explore this with myself is helpful so I don't get caught in a downward spiral that I can't get out of.

---

[3] Williams, "Disen-Whaaaat?? Understanding Disenfranchised Grief."

Wednesday, August 12, 2015

12:09 a.m.

Dear Drew,

I think it's kind of weird that I start these off with "Dear Drew." We never called each other by our names. I guess I'm doing it for that reason, and also to be consistent. You know, instead of starting it off with different things each time, like, "Hey, babe," "Baby," or "My love." Also, I have something to call this when I'm done. Whatever I'll do with it. I'm pretty tired tonight. I hope I can sleep. Last night was alright, but as soon as I tried to go to sleep, everything came down on me, and the hole came back, and I couldn't stop crying. I was feeling so small and empty and unloved. Things that only you could bring back. I think that the things that I lost when I lost you can't be found in someone or something else. The hole that is now there may never be filled, and I don't know if I want it to be. But I feel like I have to and want to find the things I had from you in myself. The love you gave me I now have to give myself. The purpose that you gave me and had for me I have to find within myself. A serious time for self-love. I just have to remember that; it is very, very hard sometimes. Especially at night. I felt you today. I know you were with me. You know the song "Ghost" By Ella Henderson? You loved that song, and I would love to hear you sing it. I think that may have been the only song you really heard me sing, or at least I let you hear me sing. And you didn't even tell me you were listening because you said if I knew you could hear my voice, I would have stopped. Which is true. Thinking about that memory today made me smile. Anyways, I was talking about you, and then that song came on the radio, and I haven't heard it in a very, very long time. Also, the sun setting sky was beautiful. So, I really think that you were in that sky looking down on me, letting me know you are here. I miss you so much. And I really wish I could tell you about these kids that I'm watching. You would laugh about how many times I have been called "Mom" from strangers when I'm with them. I wish we got to have kids someday. I'm really sorry too.

I love you, babe,

Arielle

Feel my body breathe fire

Touch my body, make life

It starts with a small flame

Made from a connection that can only be seen by the evolution of science

Delicate and intimate

Will it grow bigger?

With ease

Watch my body make life

And I'll watch the world as it is quickly destroyed

The miracle of life is literal

How two bodies can create three

How with one body can be the home of dedication

The home for creation

The institution and birthplace of strength

Because I am a human being

Because I am a woman, and life starts inside of me

My body encompasses heaven and earth to bring a piece of heaven to this earth

Nine seconds, nine minutes, nine months

How a thing of light can grow

How my body's energy knows what to do

My brain can love

And my body knows how to make the loving brain

My heart can feel

And my body knows how to create the vessel

My limbs can light fire

And my body knows my muscular blueprint

Nine months

A spark turned into a third

Nine minutes

A spark turns a forest into dust

And when it's over, when the process is through

The simple creation of something that was once not there

Is.

The simple creation of something burns into nothing

A memory

Only to be remembered by its remains

And my kin

Now parted from her place of creation

Saturday, July 25, 2015

2:00 a.m.

Dear Drew,

Today was good. I talked to my doctor, and he
cleared me for going to New Zealand. I'm going
to start looking for plane tickets and book by
next week, hopefully. Denise came and saw me
today, and we got lunch and Starbucks and
walked around the lake. Remember when you took
me there after the hospital, and I still had
my walker, and you had to help me walk on the
grass, and I put my legs across yours, and we
just sat? I remember thinking about how much
I liked you and how happy I was and how lucky
I felt that I found you. Today made me think
of that. I saw the new movie *Trainwreck* with
Thab. It was actually really funny, like I
laughed out loud, and you know that's hard for
me to do with movies. I realized that that was
the last movie I have seen since we went to
see *Fifty Shades of Grey*. I have kind of been
avoiding movies. It reminds me of you, how
much you loved going. I also talked to Deev
today. I told her how I have been feeling and
bonded with her. It was really nice. I don't
feel judged by her. I feel like she actually
listens. Mom told me about this deal Hyundai
is having, so we may go look at cars this
weekend. I think this weekend should be fun.
I am going to let it be fun. I deserve it. I
have cried enough this week; I deserve some

smiles. I miss you a lot. I wish you could have seen this movie with me. I feel like it was one where I would drag you to it, but you would have laughed a lot. I wish I could hear you laugh. I miss it so much. I loved it. I'm going to try and sleep; I have a big day tomorrow.

Love you, love you, love you,

Arielle

6

Chasing the Sun

When I think of you, I think of happiness.

I think of those people who don't know good things when they have them

And I am so sure that has never been us

You have an intimacy to you

A magnetic field that makes others not only want to trust you but to love you

The space you create is safe and warm, and I want to climb into it like I did your bed

The air and the water are softer when you're around

And after you left my room, the air had changed

Now making it a little harder to breathe without you

Because I think with my heart and feel with my body, and it can feel the void of you, and I know you are not coming back

This is me now

My hips still sore from your weight between them

The soft rock when our bodies make music

The blueprint of your body and your smell on my sheets

For that I am thankful

Thankful that you have made such an impact to my life, it has changed who I am

Thankful for the intensity that it brought to my heart, reminding myself why I am alive

Thankful that I will always love you and always think of you

You are not lost, and you will not be forgotten

I hope that if you ever feel misplaced, you can find home when you think of me

Find familiarity

Find love

Find center

Find comfort

Who you are has saved me and brought me back to life

In more ways than I can tell you

It would be such a disservice to the relationship if I did not mourn as hard as I loved

I am learning to treasure the memories

And not dwell of the future that will never be

You are a Great Love

And you deserve all the happiness I feel when I think of you

I was in desperate need of a restart button. At the time, I believe it felt more like a Hail Mary. It was mid-summer 2015 when I was in somewhat of a crisis, à la crossroad, where I thought, if I don't get a change of scenery, like *very fucking soon*, I'm scared I am going to try and kill myself. I was in deep grief that very rarely let up, and even when it did, depression was clinging to me. So, I thought of a place that I had never seen a bad picture of, safe for solo (women) travelers, and very far away from my current coordinates. New Zealand checked. I decided to go on a solo backpacking trip for six weeks, where I planned to explore both the North and South Islands. I created a flexible itinerary that included the Milford Sound, bungee jumping and skydiving in Queenstown, and a five-day, thirty-seven-mile hike through Abel Tasman National Park. As the year continued, I noticed I was having more good days and socializing more with friends and strangers, but I was by no means in a solid mental health place. Before leaving to cross the ocean on January 4, 2016, I felt like I was living in a paradoxical world. I was looking for a savior and hoping New Zealand would turn me into my own. I hoped to feel healed and changed by New Zealand, and at the same time, truly felt like I was never going to be ultimately happy again. I truly felt like I did not deserve love. I did not deserve happiness. I could never accept love from anyone else because how could I do that to Drew? I would have to learn to live my life the way it was now. Sad, lonely, and missing a piece.

When you are good at being in love with the idea of being in love

But when love hits you in the face like my hand when I find out you were never in love …

When nothing kills you slower than letting someone go

That is how you lose her.

Saturday, August 22, 2015

11:39 p.m.

Dear Drew,

I've listened to a lot of Eve 6 today. There
is a song I didn't know (I know, surprising,
right?) called "Arch Drive Goodbye," and it is
so good, and it reminds me of you, or maybe
just how I feel about you. I miss you so much.
I still get the feeling that maybe we just
haven't spoken in a long time. Or the feeling
I would get on, like, a Tuesday when I know I
had to wait three more days to see you, and it
seemed like an eternity. Now I know what it
really feels like. I just got this
overwhelming feeling of panic just now,
realizing I will never talk to you again. Holy
shit, it is hard to breathe. My heart is
broken. Beyond repair. And will always be. I
don't mean to sound pessimistic; I just think
that is the truth. Sometimes the sadness and
pain and the thoughts of you are overwhelming
and feel like they are holding me captive. I
want to let go. I want you to let me go. I
don't think it's like it's inconvenient
thinking about you or us and therefore getting
sad or having this uncontrolled pain arise
within myself. But just because it is so
powerful and it takes over my mind and body,
it is exhausting, and I feel like shit after.

I am not saying that I will stop doing this or thinking about this, or thinking about you, because I will never stop that. I just don't want it to be so controlling when it happens, for it to completely take my state of being from a safe and rational place to anywhere but that. It scares me, and it feels so fucking shitty, babe. I miss you saying, "babe" after everything. I just miss everything. I wonder what you are doing. I want you to make me laugh, tell me how much you love me and how lucky you are to have me. I want to be loved. I miss being loved by you.

Love you always, baby,

Arielle

In December 2015, I completed my degree from graduate school with a Master of Social Work with a clinical focus and passed my licensing exam on the first try. For years, I was also so impressed with myself for being in such a horrible place mentally and my world feeling like it was pulled from underneath me and still being able to accomplish all that I did during that time. But it wasn't the first time that I pulled my shit together in the final hour. My first year of graduate school was nearly as equally unpleasant as my second year. Almost to the day, a year before Drew's death, I was admitted to the hospital after having an excruciating Crohn's disease flare that quickly turned into a thirty-day affair. I endured medical trauma that changed me physically, mentally, emotionally, and spiritually. The trauma and grief that I continue to experience from March 3, 2014 to April 2, 2014 has forced me to invite more flexibility into my life. During that time, I had to leave my job, put school on hold, and was forced to focus on my health and, quite frankly, fight for my life. This led me to postpone my degree by a semester and my walk across the stage at my graduation by a year. Though my degree was in social work, I feel like I must have double majored in adaptability, as I saw myself becoming more resilient in future scenarios. So, it wasn't a surprise when I once had a medium tell me that I've perfected picking up, going, and changing the flow of things, especially in my career. True.

Presently, as a psychotherapist specializing in grief and trauma, I am reminded of this period in my life—how amazing it felt to do so well in some areas, while others, like my mental health, were gasping for air. I can identify that during this time of grief and trauma, I had to find ways to cope. What I know now is that individuals with traumatic stress or PTSD could be prone to channeling uncomfortable or unresolved feelings into their work or schoolwork. It is used as an emotional regulator that stimulates a sense of control and stability when much of life feels out of control and traumatic. It can also give us purpose that can become almost addictive, especially if there has been a loss of purpose or identity.[1] It now makes sense to me that I would strive for overachievement, create high expectations for myself, and take on perfectionistic

---

[1] Paperny, "Do Some Trauma Survivors Cope by Overworking?"

qualities. Though there may have been many times that I subconsciously did this to avoid emotions, I see this as a survival skill, especially because during that time, it took copious amounts of energy to get through each day.

I felt more than ready to start the trip that, unknowingly at the time, changed my life. After proudly only having two "oh, shit" moments before even entering New Zealand, I embraced the anxious energy inside of myself that immediately got me lost in city center Auckland looking for my first hostel. I gave myself a flexible itinerary to provide some structure, but anyone who has solo traveled before knows, some of the best moments happen when you just say yes. I was fully entranced by the country and falling more and more in love with not only New Zealand's distinct level of biodiversity but the presence of those around me who called these two islands home and those who were there for a transient immersion. It took me a while to warm up, but I soon was Ms. Social Butterfly and found that the beating heart of my trip were the people I met.

I lean against you, my protector

Emotionally and physically supporting my being

You embody a maternal caregiver, holding me as I hug you back

So big, bold, and beautiful. You provide me shade from the harshness of the elements and the harshness of the world

I watch the clouds dance between your extremities, almost so intimately that I start to blush

I am a guest in your presence as you are just as alive as I am

Generations away from Grandmother Willow, yet still holding the wisdom that is rooted within

I have touched a tree before, but now feeling your aged bark against my hands

Like it is skin that has gone dry from lack of attention and care

The intimate experience of putting my hands on you

Remembering a body I used to know

About halfway through my trip, I spent a few nights in Kaikōura, a beach town on the coast of the South Island. I was staying in a hostel on my second night there. I was in the kitchen making dinner in my University of Maryland School of Social Work Sweatshirt when I heard, "Hey! I go there!" I looked up, and in front of me was a guy that looked around nineteen or twenty years old, smiling at me with a surprised look on his face. "What?" I replied. Just then, a girl walked up behind him and shouted, "Oh my God, we go there!" Here we are, 8,849 miles away from Maryland, meeting in the kitchen of Fish Tank Lodge, bonded by the same university. Their names were Samantha and Ryan, two friends who decided to hop over to New Zealand before starting a semester abroad in Australia. They told me they went to the College Park campus of University of Maryland, while I attended the school of social work on the Baltimore campus, where the professional schools were located. We hung out that night and quickly, as travelers do, grew a friendship. I told them that the next day I was off to my next destination of Christchurch via InterCity Bus, and they told me they were heading to the same town, offering me a ride in the car they had. Remembering that this is not only what solo traveling was all about—*saying yes*—but it would be cool to save some money and time by cancelling my bus reservation. I was grateful. We all woke up the next morning before the sun to walk across the street to the beach to see the most beautiful sunrise together. Enjoying the calm beauty and the cool air, we all sat on the beach making rock formations and soaking in the life we chose.

Later that morning, we packed up and headed for Christchurch, making a very important stop at Kaikōura's seal colony to catch some rays and snap a seal selfie. The two-and-a-half-hour drive along the coast to the oldest city in New Zealand was nothing short of majestic. Samantha and Ryan dropped me off at my hostel before heading to theirs, with a plan to meet up later that evening. Disappointingly, I got a text a little later saying that they were tired from the day and passing out early. The next time I would see those rascals would be in late November that year when we got together for dinner back in Maryland, reminiscing about the past eleven months.

I used Christchurch as a "filler destination," one of those places to go that had available bus and hostel spots left when you needed to fill a gap in the schedule. I didn't plan on staying more than a night and didn't know where I was headed to next. With my day now freed up, I thought I should take the time to do a little planning. After settling into my eight-bed all-gender room, I collected my map, notes, and Kindle and planted myself on a couch downstairs in the lobby-turned-cafe. The first of a long series of events that would change my life happened soon after sitting down.

Even when my heart breaks

Your hands are big enough to catch the pieces before they shatter on the ground forever

After coming up empty when looking for a way out of Christchurch the next day and not having a bed to sleep in if I had to extend my stay, I am *stressed.* Heavily focused and sure that I'm on the brink of an anxiety attack, a man walks up on my right side and sits across from me on the opposing couch. Now to set the scene, this good-size room that was full of seating options was completely empty, so my first thought was, *"Really? You need to sit here?"* After discretely witnessing me vigorously throw around pages of notes, turning my map around approximately four hundred times in angst, he could tell I was in a frenzy.

"Planning your trip?" he asks.

"Well, I'm trying," I say, "but nothing is available, and there are no buses available anywhere close to here, and I have no idea where I'm going to sleep tomorrow night, and I don't know what I'm going to do, and this is so stupid and frustrating!" Within seconds, I regress back into a thirteen-year-old with minimal brain function and zero ability to control my emotions because the world hates me. *How amazing!*

"Don't worry," he says. "Everything is going to work out."

Transforming back to my twenty-four-year-old self, I accept the help offered from this patient man and find a bus leaving at six o'clock the next morning. We end up talking for hours on those couches when he decides to ditch his plans to attend a street festival and instead lean into a connection found with a stranger. When writing this, I asked him if he preferred me using his real name or a pseudonym, and if so, what should I call him? Quickly, he responded with "Mr. Nice Guy."

Mr. Nice Guy was a successful and youthful forty-three-year-old, divorced father of three on a sabbatical from his life as well. He was living a life of complete predictability and lacked the nomadic escape he was thirsty for. We opened up fast to each other, and I was soon grateful for his seat selection. As it got closer to dinnertime, he asked if I "wanted to go get some grub." There was a hesitancy, not knowing if it was the right decision to continue my evening with him, but I took a chance on him and myself and said yes. I went back to my room to change into jeans from my athletic shorts and spritzed some perfume along my collar bone. We ate at a Thai restaurant and walked around the city until we were mesmerized by a glowing pier, coaxing us to walk the beach below. We walked and talked, hoping secretly the night wouldn't end. We found some driftwood by the pier and sat next to each other, sometimes enjoying each other's voices and sometimes enjoying the silence.

For years, I have been doing this thing I call *1, 2, 3, go*. If I ever feel afraid or nervous to do something and need a quick dose of courage, I can say, "1 ... 2 ... 3 ... " and still back out. But if I make it to "go," I have to do it. It's a vow I make to myself, and I have never not followed through. So, on that night, feeling more accessible and alive than I have felt in almost a year, I said to myself, "1 ... 2 ... 3 ... go."

And then out loud, "Can I kiss you?"

Turns out Mr. Nice Guy's real name is Mr. Nice Kisser.

Around midnight or so, we walk through the town and head back to the hostel. I mention that I will be getting very minimal hours of sleep after the night we had and have to catch a 6:00 a.m. bus at a station I have yet to locate. Mr. Nice Guy says that he has a car and offers to drive me to the bus station in the morning. I tell him how awfully nice of him it is to offer, and first decline, but then remember that it's okay to let people help you, and I graciously accept. After a full afternoon-to-evening hang, future island destinations and plans were surely shared. My next planned activity was about six days away in one of the most northern parts of the South Island, Abel Tasman National Park. While we are walking up the stairs to the second floor where the bedrooms are located, he takes the leap and says, "Actually, I'm heading north and could just drop you off for your hike in Abel Tasman if you wanted to travel together for a bit." I had a decision to make in the next two seconds ... and weirdly enough, I remember all of this going through my head in those two seconds. If I say yes, I'm going to have sex with this person. Do I want to have sex with him? We're adults and had a *moment* of an evening. We both know what's up.

A genuinely hopeful and excited smile rolls across my face. "Hell yes."

We go our separate ways for the night, and the next morning, we depart on what would become the next chapter of my life.

This was where the biggest dialectic in my grief was learned. The amount of time Mr. Nice Guy and I spent together in New Zealand remains one of the most beautiful, loving, and joyful times of my life. I felt resurrected from the deep hole that grief directed me into. I fell in love. Mr. Nice Guy's medicinal energy helped me heal from what I had believed unmendable. He modeled safety in vulnerability, showing me that I could be vulnerable with him and myself. Looking back on our first night of traveling together, our bodies wrapped around each other, I let him hold me, touch me, and for the first time since Drew, allow him to see me for who I was: cracked, heartbroken, lonely. And through letting someone in, my heart started to repair because he wasn't afraid of the broken pieces and showed me I could become powerful in my grief. He gave me hope for myself, which at the time was a foreign concept. And I learned this: Not letting myself absorb love or show love was a self-inflicted punishment that did nothing but keep me stagnant in my grief. I can have joy and love in my life and still mourn the loss of Drew. Giving and accepting love and intimacy from someone does not mean that I have forgotten about Drew. It proves that through showing vulnerability and leaning into the pain of loss, you can come out a stronger, loving, resilient, and more grateful person.

Mr. Nice Guy has played a monumental role in finding acceptance of Drew's death and, more critically, befriending myself again in the process. I was stuck in an incredibly lonely state of unforgiveness. In the most wholeheartedly caring and cultivating way, never wanting to replace Drew, Mr. Nice Guy became a part of my life that was only possible when I found love for myself. His passionate appetite for life was contagious. Continuing consistent contact with each other even after we parted ways in New Zealand eventually landed me in Austin, Texas. This was a radical Plan B that showed up as I was waiting for my visa to get approved in efforts to move to New Zealand. While holding my breath on immigration, I went to visit Mr. Nice Guy in Austin, where he was living. Knowing that he had his own plans on leaving the blue oasis and moving to California, I thought that if New Zealand didn't work out, Austin just might be the next move. After four months of back-and-forth communication, New Zealand immigration declined my visa due to medical reasons, and I was devastated. Heartbroken loss that I thought I had become so accustomed to hits differently every time and introduced me to a new kind of grief. Handicapped by a medication that sustains my livelihood, continuously living that dialectical-charmed kinda life. New Zealand is the one that got away, and I will never not be infatuated with her, feeling confident we will be together again one day.

My throat is closing

My lungs fill with water

Like his.

I can't stay in environments cold and contained

I'm not running

I just don't want to

Suffocating on regularity

My hometown is taking the life out of me

I dream of dancing on colors

Grabbing the joy radiating from the sweat on the face beside me

But I'm not running

Just dancing away

I'm flipping the page

No, changing the book

Switching genres

Refusing to be a tragedy

Hear me when I tell you

Hardship to acceptance

But remember, I'm not running

I'm gracefully walking out the door

Because when I walked out the door and the cold air hit like whips on my chest

I think, this is not weather

These are the chains that I have to Houdini out of if I do not wish to drown in this tank

How could I run?

Losing and leaving the lovers that leached on to my life

My screaming heart made no noise to ears to blind to see

So, I am leaving to a place I know I can feel

Make sure you miss me

Like you will miss your home

Home is missing him

Missing him like air

So, I'm running like I care

Maryland, and more specifically Baltimore, became an almanac of loss. Being in a place that in many ways still felt like home was now blemished with memories that held pain and lost love. Feeling like I was living in a contradiction, a place that I had grown to love also felt tarnished in an unfixable way. After the rejection from immigration, I decided I was going to work the summer in Maryland and then move to Austin by the end of the year. I found a roommate on Craigslist, and we found an apartment. I didn't have a job and expected not to know anyone, as the only person I knew there was Mr. Nice Guy, who said he was escaping the heat to the beachy west coast. Turns out, though, he stuck around and made my transition to Austin smooth, to say the least.

When Drew died, my life split into two parts: before and after. It's strange to have built a life in Austin that doesn't include anyone who knew Drew or knew me when I was with Drew. They don't know the person who I was before I met Drew or who we were together. They are only able to know the aftermath. What grief has done to me and who it has made me turn into. The version of me that can only show pictures and tell stories. It makes me sad that my life in Austin and the people I have met and added to my chosen family won't ever see the vibrant, energetic connection Drew and I had. And they also didn't see the person that would wake up screaming and crying in emotional and somatic pain during that first year … though it's not like it ended completely after the one-year mark. I noticed that when I think about my life from a larger perspective, I automatically endorse the split, and it becomes a point of reference. *Did I meet them before or after Drew died? Did I start that job when we were together or after he died? I moved to Austin after Drew passed away.* Everything is now before and after. The middle is him.

I want to live in a world where people smile and mean it

A world where people listen and not just think about their next response

And when I tell you I love you, you tell me you love me too

Not because you feel obligated but because you feel liberated

I want to live in a world where maybe means yes

And I choose honesty over politeness

And "carpe diem" isn't a saying on a shirt but a hard-learned way of life

Because you were always meant to seize your own loneliness

Seize your own loveliness

And when you do, you wonder what other treasures you're hiding from yourself

I want to live in a world where girls are born encouraged

Encouraged to find their own beauty, romance, and confidence from within

And when the hurt comes, and believe me, baby, it will come

You will be grateful and not fearful

Revitalized and not disheartened

And you summon the courage to console yourself

And one day the world you imagined is the world you build

The world you live

My introduction to life in Austin was spritzed with love and joy being with Mr. Nice Guy. A new type of relationship for both of us that we cherished deeply arrived at its planned expiration date on June 1, 2017, when the move to California came to fruition. It was strange to be in a relationship with a person for a known amount of time, as most of us don't experience romance that way. Though I believe that it encouraged us to truly treasure the time we had together, and it helped me stay present even when my trauma symptoms of abandonment and worry kicked in. The gratitude I felt in this relationship could only be possible for me to have after experiencing such a great loss of a partner before. When I was with Drew, I knew how lucky I was. I knew what I had when I had it. And similarly, with Mr. Nice Guy, we were mindful of the unconventional love and bond we shared, something I believe a lot of people don't experience. So, when the breakup came, once again, it was significantly painful because it was a significant love.

Maybe it is too painful for you to tell me to stop contacting you

    So, you keep it short

And every time I text, you take a breath

    Hoping I will take a hint

<u>*Telling me to leave you alone will be a heartbreak like you've never felt*</u>

And I don't know what is worse

    You keeping it short

Or me knowing why you do, and I still respond

...

I want to make a life with you

    You need to stay first

I'm tired of my heart breaking into pieces

    So painfully in love with you

Don't wait for your head to speak the same language as your heart

    It will never be literate.

Grieving the loss of the relationship with Mr. Nice Guy has been continuous. It wasn't a clean break, and contact continued a while afterwards. Eventually, our roles in each other's lives became more distinct, and the distance grew appropriately. Secondary loss appeared again in many forms because it was not just the loss of the relationship but a loss of the person who was such an intricate part of the recovery from my world of grief. To lose another person who played such a vital role in my life was gut-wrenching. If he helped me with Drew, who was going to help me with him? The answer to this was already within me. So, I dug deeper and remembered that I have been in great heartache before. And I asked myself, *"How do you move through this?"*

You cut yourself some slack. You forgive yourself for not knowing what you didn't know before you learned it. And you tell yourself you will have a lot of shitty days, but over time, they will become less frequent and less debilitating. You surround yourself with people who show up for you, *and only the people who show up for you.* And you learn to love yourself in this new form, missing pieces and all. You are resilient because there isn't another choice. And you are good to yourself, in *every* way possible.

How dare you

How dare you come back and not even know that the words you say stab me again and again when you say you love me but now touch her

How dare you bring her into the space that was ours, a town that was ours, a life that was ours

Who is this imposter you call your love, because she is not me

She stole my life with you, and it was a life that was hidden, but it was real to me

Part of yours and all of mine, don't you know?!

Don't you know how hard my heart breaks knowing that this life you have now was once mine, but I have been replaced with an older, more appropriate model

How dare you move on, like you have the right to, even if you do

Because my heart hasn't, and it has cracked and healed over and over and over again, and when I know you are back breathing the same air, I stop

How dare you think that the love I have given you isn't the purest, most vulnerable thing you have ever received, because if you question that, I won't be able to breathe

When I love, I love fully, wholeheartedly

How dare you be happy when I am still broken from your love being taken away

How dare you not see my broken heart when you look at me

Can't you see through my eyes into my soul that wants you so bad my body aches

You don't

Your eyes are preoccupied

While mine only watch

Monday, February 20, 2017

10:49 p.m.

Dear Drew,

It's been over a year since I last wrote to you. I can't believe that. So many things have happened, but it's not like you don't know that. I know you see me and how my life is. I'm writing a book. Well, I guess I have started the process of thinking about writing a book. I know what it is going to be called and what it will be about. I was thinking of a combination of stories/essays, poems, and these letters. I guess I will have to reread each one to find the ones that I want to put in the book. I have been thinking a lot about it but not doing it because I know it will be painful. Stalling, once again. I have been wanting to write to you for a while. About a couple of weeks or so. I don't know what has taken me so long. If I'm being honest with myself, it's probably a mixture of laziness, feeling scared, and forgetting. I'm sorry for that. But I guess I now believe that I don't need to write to you for you to hear me, or for you to know what I'm doing, even though it's still a nice thing to do. Tonight, though, something happened that I have been dreading since you died almost two years ago. I just stopped writing for a moment there, staring at "almost two years ago." It doesn't seem real. That's so long without you, babe.

I'm now crying. I don't cry about you often anymore. The membrane is getting thicker. Well, I just got off the phone with my friend Ashley, who I met speaking to Professor Gold's class. Man, I wish you could have met her; she is the sweetest girl with a beautiful heart. You would have liked her a lot. I tell her that all the time. Anyway, we were catching up, and I got off the phone and went to Snapchat to see if there is anyone in my phone book who I want to add. I can't remember the last time I did this; it's been a long time. I obviously still have your number in my phone. That's not going to come out. I scroll down the list, and there it is, your name. Well, actually, it's "Daddy Warbucks Weston," never changed it back. And underneath, it has a username. And next to it, a moving picture of a boy, and it's not you. What's weird is that he resembles a younger version of you. Just with glasses. My hand and body froze when I saw it, and I just looked at it. It finally happened; your phone number was given to another person. The domino effect in my mind is endless, but it means that it is no longer yours. If I were to text or call it, someone would answer, but it wouldn't be you. I'm not going to do that. I miss you so much. I haven't had a big cry about you in a while, so in a way, this feels good. My heart, though, is hurting badly right now, feeling very heavy with sadness. I wish you could see my life now. See how happy I am and how well I am doing. I moved to Austin. I live in fucking

Texas; can you believe that shit? The truth is, though, I love it. I just packed my car and left Maryland with my mom, and we drove down here, and she dropped me off. It's been hard living there for a while now, babe, and I just needed a change. There's something else I want to tell you, like officially, in writing. I feel weird even typing this because I know you already know. I have a boyfriend. It just happened last week, actually "officially" a week ago today. I feel stupid for saying that to you just now, but I somehow feel like it is important to have a timeline with you. It's someone I never expected. His name is Mr. Nice Guy. He's 44. He has three kids that are older, like almost my age, older. So, it's a little uncomfortable in a way, new territory I've never experienced. But, babe, I love him. So much. We care a lot about each other. He takes care of me the way I deserve to be taken care of, and I know you want that for me. He loves me and wants the best for me in every way possible. He reminds me a lot of you. You have similar hearts. And I feel you when I'm with him. I really think you sent him to me. I wholeheartedly believe that. Thank you. He is wonderful and makes me very happy, and I am so thankful he is in my life at this time. I feel vulnerable using the word boyfriend with him because I feel like that word is forever reserved for you. That probably sounds ridiculous, but part of me does feel that way. Even so, I am proud and happy to call him my boyfriend. Because I know he respects that title, and he respects you and who you are to me and how you will always be in my life and a part of me. It's part of the reason why I love him. When we first met, he told me, "Everything is going to work out." It reminded me of when you would say, "Don't worry. Everything is going to be amazing." It hurts a lot writing to you tonight. I have cried through most of writing this, but I want to tell you that everything is amazing. My life is great and better than I ever could have imagined it a year ago. I feel very lucky. And I am finally very happy.

Thanks, babe. I love you, and I miss you so much,

Arielle

7

This is a Love Story

I often think about the last time I was in love

I look fondly at her, knowing that we are deeply different people now

Who I am now has never been in love

My serpent skin had shed

As did the hair on my head

I wonder what my current being might look like when she is in love

I imagine she stands taller

Her spine heavier with wisdom

And sturdier with conviction

There have been too many changes in life

Too many growth spurts that have been too painful to have happened without flourish

It seems impossible for me to love in the same way that I have before

I hope for the unfamiliar

I sense I would love with a vengeance

An encompassing power that is filled with a maturity

Even who I stand to be in this moment

Is different than who I will be when I let the words intentionally slip

Learning the dance of how to love myself has become muscle memory

And still picking up the new moves of revised music to loving another

Both age like fine red wine

I knew it was coming before he said it. We are lying in bed, still breathing in each other's pheromones, high on oxytocin. Drew moves closer and koalas his leg around my body, holding himself up above me with his ever-growing triceps. He looks into my eyes, and I know it's about to happen. I hold my breath.

In a loving and calmly nervous voice, Drew says, "I love you."

I knew he meant it. And all these years later, humorously with credence, I stand by my response.

"I love that you love me."

Whether it was the women Drew told at his work to try and get some advice on the situation or the friends I told soon after or anytime I'm repeating this story, the most common reaction to this is "Ouch." I always have to laugh, though, because what I said was very intentional. I *did* love that he loved me, and I was so close to being sure I loved him at the time, and yet, I wanted to be 100% positive. He didn't say it again after that, which was okay because I knew he was burned. It wasn't until we were back on the East Coast from our cross-country road trip, in a shitty Virginia hotel for the night, that the words were spoken. Fortuitously, in a similar manner, lying next to each other in bed, I spoke what I then knew I had been feeling for so long.

"Hey ... I love you."

Drew smiles and replies, "I love that you love me."

We both laugh lusciously, and he tells me, "I knew you were going to say that just now. I love you too."

It felt like we were just at the beginning of a long lifetime partnership together. This was it. We found each other. It felt like at the time, we both were taking nothing for granted while still being aware of our vulnerabilities. Adventitiously, we were in the middle. Now closing in on what, in hindsight, would be the start of red flags and the things I would feel the guilty weight of and relive for years. Small inconsistencies that I subconsciously put in the box of denial, things I wouldn't allow myself to see because it didn't match the narrative that we had built and I was still very much engaged in. I could not have done anything differently because of this truth, though still attached to the responsibility that was never mine to have.

One of these times was in August 2014 when I was on vacation in Asheville with my family. We were walking around town when Drew called me and said he relapsed, using alcohol, marijuana, and cocaine. I stopped in my tracks as he told me he didn't understand why other people could drink casually, even do drugs casually, but he couldn't. That he's never tried to do these things with a known stopping point in mind, and he said he "just wanted to be sure." Drew told me he was going to go to Ocean City to spend time with Tyler and Digges to get out of Baltimore until I got back. I was so confused; how could he slip like this? Wasn't everything good? I was furious. Retrospectively, I didn't know how to communicate the level of threat, alarm, and panic I felt.

I was yelling, "You wanted to make sure?! That is such bullshit. You already know that isn't you. You already know that you can't do that and just stop. You are so much smarter than that, so don't use that for a sorry excuse. If you wanted to do it, just take responsibility. How *dare* you do this to yourself! How dare you do this to *me*! You could have fucking died! What would I do then?! What if we had kids and you did that? What would happen then? What if you died, and I was left with these fucking kids all by myself? You never thought about that. What the fuck would I do if you die?!"

My pain repressed a lot of this memory, now having to work to bring it back to consciousness. I feel shameful for the way I reacted. That's just it, though; I reacted, not responded. The thought of losing him was so excruciating, it triggered hurtful words. I wish I could take them back and instead express my anger and hurt but in a more compassionate way. The last part of what I said to him has haunted me for many years after Drew's death. Because that ended up a reality in the end. I found out what I would do if he died. I would survive.

I have found my superpower

Discovering that it has been there all along

Maturing over time and becoming stronger and sturdier within myself

I have been through deeply painful things

Still not intimidated as I walk towards more

In myself

In others

This is part of who I am—centering me in my devotion to authenticity

The death was a catalyst

Forcing me to observe all the others that landed me here

The death was the last impetus

My ancestral blood spins a thread of survivorship

No short of a miracle

I really started to find my survivorship when I shared my grief with others. I first saw this when starting the GRASP support group, and it led me to find power in connection. I wanted to do more of this and found other outlets to share my experience in a way that was raw and real. If I moved through vulnerability by sharing the truth of my grief, I found that I connected with people in a way I never had before and that this was a powerful space. I was already speaking at Towson University a few times a year, talking about graduate school, internships, and experiences I had, in efforts to provide guidance to the students interested in continuing their education in the social work field. When Drew passed away, I adjusted my speaking topics and added speaking about resilience— à la what do you do when shit hits the fan in your life? I also became inspired by Hannah, who was writing and submitting essays and articles to online platforms. I thought this might be a good expression for myself as well, and for the first time, my own words left a Word document and moved into the public eye. It was cathartic and validating to write about Drew and my grief, as it is now. I wrote about pain and anniversaries, like in *The Gifts of Grief* and *Six Months*. And about the trickiness of what grief will have you believe, like in, *I Know What You're Thinking, Don't I?* And of course, about New Zealand in, *The Chicken Nugget Diet*. Hoping ... knowing ... that I couldn't be the only one feeling the way I was and that this was the start of something bigger.

Thursday, August 6, 2015

12:06 a.m.

Dear Drew,

As I write this, it is August 6, a little past midnight. Today is five months since you died. And those words still get me. Sometimes when I write to you, it just feels like I'm writing to myself, like a journal entry. Maybe this is what that is. It's not like I will ever send you these letters. Somehow, I hope you still read them. I miss you so, so much. Nediva and I went out tonight for dinner at Fleet Street Kitchen for restaurant week. We looked super cute, and I know you would have loved my outfit. I was feeling good. You would have thought I looked really hot. I wanted to send you a picture of me the entire night, just so I could get a text back saying how beautiful I was. I miss that so much. I miss hearing I'm beautiful, from your lips. I miss your voice. When I think about it, I cry. As I write this, the hole comes back. It's big tonight, babe. My heart aches and is in so much pain. It is overwhelming.

Five months of not hearing your voice, not seeing your lips move, not having those lips touch mine. Five months since my life went up in flames and my heart caved in. It's hard to write tonight. I just keep crying. I still think it's not real. How can this be real? How can this be my life? How can your life be over and mine still continue now with this shadow forever over it and the pain always in it? I can't believe we won't create any more memories together. And that all the memories that I have in my head or the pictures that we took are the only ones I will ever get. That's hard to swallow. It doesn't feel real, babe. I don't want it to be real. I want to wake up, and you will be next to me, and I want to tell you about the horrible dream I just had. I just want to tell you something, anything. I am so sad. So, so, so fucking sad. Depending on the weather on Friday, I think I am going to try and go to the cemetery. I don't really know what to say tonight. I am just really, really sad. Nediva and I were talking about the future a little, and I said that the path I thought I would have, I don't know if I want it anymore; I don't know if I will be satisfied, if it will be good enough for me. I need something that will make my soul happy. I was thinking about motivational speaking. I think I would be really good at it, and you would be proud of me. I want to talk about resiliency. I think it would be a good way to honor you because you were so amazing at it at the meetings. You captured a room like I have never seen, and you were so articulate in doing so. It was really spectacular. I hope to be as good as you, but in the meantime, you are really good motivation. I guess I'll look into this more and write more about it soon.

I'm getting tired. Stay with me while I sleep.
I want to know you are next to me, even still.

I love that you love me,

Arielle

I continued to connect myself to individuals who created platforms of their own. I was lucky enough to be interviewed by a handful of podcast hosts who valued talking about grief, mental health, and trauma in the same way I did. I noticed that within my own social circle, I started to become the person who friends saw as the "grief expert," referring people they knew to informally talk with me about their experience of loss. This was an energizing way to honor Drew, naturally being the supportive ear to help them through their grief process.

I was seeking more prominent platforms to share my story and continue to process and explore my grief and how it has changed over the years, healing myself by healing others. I had the amazing opportunity to perform at Bedpost Confessions, a live storytelling show about sex, sexuality, and gender, in January 2019 to an audience of over three hundred people each of the three running nights. At the time, I had also been submitting proposals and applications to TEDx Talks all over the country. A few months later, April 2, I dropped to the ground crying with gratitude when I received an email welcoming me to the TEDx stage in Colorado Springs. The other speakers and I had an incredibly tight window to write, practice, and memorize our eight-to-fifteen-minute speech. Thankfully, I had already written my speech and started to memorize it, because even though I didn't know how long it would take, I was going to get myself on that stage. On May 12, 2019, I took the stage and became a TEDx speaker. I wish I could say that it was a positive and amazing experience, but it wasn't. Before that day, I had perfected my speech. I felt confident and excited and thankful to have the opportunity to share the *stage of stages* with so many other sensational speakers. But that day, my body was in physical pain, I skipped over an entire paragraph, and I didn't feel Drew with me. I walked off the stage into the wing where another speaker whom I became close to was waiting for me with open arms and a big smile on her face. Instead of allowing myself the joy of this momentous accomplishment, I immediately burst into tears, repeating, "I fucked up. I fucked up." Two event volunteers followed me into the green room to console me and give me some perspective. They asked me what my "why" was for doing a TEDx talk.

I shared, "Because I want people to know they aren't alone. Know that Drew existed, and he was loved, and I loved him, and he is so much more than what killed him."

One of them asked, "Was that taken away when you didn't say that paragraph?"

"No."

With compassion, one of them asked, "What would you tell someone you love if this happened to them?"

Wiping tears from my face, "That it's okay and it doesn't matter. I still did that."

Sharing this experience with others is important to me because in a world where we often see a small, curated view of a person's life, realistic and relatable behind-the-scenes truths are rarely told. If you watch my TEDx Talk, I imagine most people cannot detect the "mess up." You also won't detect the emotional or physical pain I was in at the time. So, I am letting it be known in writing. It was a painful experience that made me feel immense shame for weeks because of it, *and* I achieved a large goal of mine which will forever be available for others to see and use as a resource. I love myself, I forgive myself, and I'm proud of myself.

What started as reciprocated support with someone in a Facebook group soon stimulated something that encapsulated a way of life. Connecting authentically with others by sharing experiences became the birthplace of what would later shape the therapeutic space I built for and with clients in my practice. Grief can feel like it takes everything you have. So, when my clients come to the space that is foundationally constructed on empowerment, there will be hope found. Naturally slipping into the role and career of being a grief and trauma therapist has been one of the biggest honors of my life. It has allowed me to celebrate Drew in a way that continues his legacy by helping others through some of the most painful moments of their lives. I've found purpose, grace, and dedication in unequivocal loss—who would have thought?

There is a bond

Invisible and stronger than steel

This is to my sisters

Thinking about who you have become and watching you grow

Following my age

I hope you take with you everything you can carry

And what you can't carry in your heart, you don't need

You inspire me to be more than everything I thought I could be

Because I look to you and see the demands the world has put on you

And you take those demands and keep going, keep walking

Keeping your head high

The world will not always be kind

And people may not always be kind

And the ones you love may not always be kind

But know that now and when wrinkles cover your skin

I make the promise to be your light and your guide

To be the footsteps left behind

My heart aches when I tell you how much I love you

But I simply can't put it into words

So, I leave this here for you.

Monday, October 14, 2019

9:25 p.m.

Dear Drew,

It has really been a while. I know I have
written to you since that last entry....I am
not sure where it is. Probably in a different
document. I'm in bed lying with your blanket,
on your birthday. You would have been twenty-
nine today. I posted this picture of you as a
kid, maybe ten years old. You look like you
were at a friend's birthday party. I felt okay
all day, off, a little depressed and generally
sad. But when I saw that picture, damn, it
really got me. You just looked so cute and
happy; you could see it in your eyes. And it
made me immediately think about the kids we
would have had together. How they would have
looked just like you. I don't know if I ever
told you that ... that I always imagined our
kids to look more like you. I don't really
know why. Maybe it's because you had strong
features. I miss them. The kids we never had.
Isn't that crazy? I really do miss them. As if
they existed and then they were also taken
away. I think that is still one of the things
I grieve heavily ... the kids we were going to
have. The kids we would talk about. The kids
that I would be mean to, and you would be fun,
and they knew they could get away with stuff
with you, right? Remember? The more I think
about it, the more it makes sense. Not only am

I now thinking about kids in general, feeling that clock, I guess, but also, if I am grieving children, I would imagine that is grief that really lasts, maybe forever. I talked to your mom tonight. It was hard. She is going through so much right now, things I can't imagine, but I just felt like I had no energy to give her. Like I ran out of words and empathy and energy for other people. Today took more from me than I thought and than I had planned, ha. I'm wearing your boxers to sleep tonight. To be closer to you.

I also just took a pause in writing to find where those other letters went....I found them, never fear. The last time I wrote you was in 2017, so yeah, it's been a hot minute. On the two-year anniversary of your death. Now, four and a half years after you died, it's your twenty-ninth birthday, and here I am again. The last time I wrote you, I was in such a different place. I was in love. I was in a job that I didn't like. And I was still pretty new to Austin. Mr. Nice Guy, the boyfriend I told you about, we broke up. I guess you knew that without me having to officially tell you. It was hard, and if I am being honest, it still is. I almost texted him just now. To tell him that I am reading over these letters, and I reread the one where I told you about him. I miss him so much, two and a half years after the breakup. That's what happens with great loves, I guess. I know I shouldn't, and I won't. But what really keeps me from doing it is the thought of *what if he is married*? I still don't feel strong enough to hear that. I still feel too lonely. That's a real bitch these days. The loneliness. The Band-Aids in and out of my life, maybe for a night, maybe for longer ... and eventually, I don't need them anymore. I miss feeling loved. I miss having someone who understands me and wants me the way I want them. Hard to find, apparently. In one of my other letters, I write that writing to you is like a timeline. I am really feeling that. Not only a timeline of missing you and the grief but a timeline of my life. Where I was, what I was doing, how I was feeling. I have accomplished a lot since the last time I wrote. I am really working on my speaking career, and I started collecting research for that book that I have been writing for years now ... very slowly. But I have had a lot of other speaking experiences and career uplifts. A TEDx Talk, podcasts, classrooms. I'm working on hopefully my first paid speaking gig at this temple here. You would be so proud. And you would feel famous. I feel so honored to talk about you, tell people who you were and how you helped others. That's all I want to do. And I do that; I know I do. People come to me now if they need help. I take others under my wing who are injured from the same thing as I was. It fills me with joy and makes me feel very purposeful. I don't know if I can ask you for things, but I'm guessing it wouldn't hurt. I feel like my depression has been kind of bad lately. I think it's a mixture of stress at work, being lonely, and not having a good work-life balance. I am just so tired all the time. I also have this belief that has come up for me time and time again of "I'm not good enough, and I'm not doing enough." I know I am great, and I am doing a lot. I have a lot to be proud of, and I have put a lot in perspective, but I still feel it sometimes. So, I guess I am asking for things to feel easier. Not even necessarily get easier but just help me feel like I can manage it better. And maybe help me with this loneliness thing. But only if it will end up okay....I am tired of wasting time. Make it good, babe. I just felt like in the last minute, multiple signs came to me, so I want to believe you're listening. I feel like I am getting distracted, so I think I am going to end it here. I also had twenty-nine trees planted for you from the Arbor Day Foundation, like I have been doing the past couple of years. I sent the card to your mom so she can have it and know about it. I think it may make her happy. I miss you so much, and I wish we could be living this life together, in love, healthily, honestly. Don't know if that would be possible, but I like to think it could be. Happy birthday.

I love you with my whole heart,

Arielle

Intermission

〰

Whisky Tango Foxtrot

I found my creative flow after almost a year and a half of either trying to force magic out of myself that just wasn't available yet or backing away from writing altogether. I found the flow again at the beginning of quarantine during the COVID-19 pandemic. This surprised me at the time because just like many others, I was in an uncomfortable place of uncertainty. Looking back, the contagion forced people into an environment where loss, trauma, and change became more familiar all around the world, and to be frank, it's my cup of tea to write about. Maybe I shouldn't have been surprised because it finally gave me the chance to slow down, the space to create without the pressure of satisfying the parts of me that wanted to go out, drink, or spend money. Instead, I focused on what I love to do and explored my own ambition by metamorphosing until it turned into magic, or at least what I perceive to be magic.

In 2020, the world became fluent in the language of crisis. We saw the extremes of humanity that could only be called out in calamitous circumstances. It would feel neglectful of responsibility to pass by the losses that the world as a whole and individually experienced. Furthermore, as this book is written, we are in a time where the United States and most definitely the world is by no means back to "normal," and a lot of us continue to grieve the aftermath of losses. The worldwide spread of coronavirus led to what I believe will be known as one of the largest examples of collective grief the living world will experience. Collective grief is defined as grief that is felt by a group, such as a community, society, or nation, as the outcome of an event that resulted in casualties or deep tragedy.[1] Familiar examples of this would be the September 11 terrorist attacks, Hurricane Katrina, and the Columbine High School Shootings. In addition, cumulative grief became familiar to many of us as well. Think of this as a "grief overload": when we haven't finished grieving an initial loss and a second loss is then experienced.[2] For many people, this was their first time experiencing either or both, collective and cumulative loss.

In the most basic sense, we lost what we thought our life would look like every day. Most of those who were lucky enough to keep their jobs sold out Amazon, Wayfair, and Target ordering desks and chairs to set up in their home. We added "Zoom" before the things we used to do in person: Zoom work meetings, Zoom dates, Zoom wine nights, Zoom weddings, Zoom baby showers. We changed the way we grieved and connected. No longer able to hold and embrace each other in support and love when we felt alone, suffered another loss, or simply just had a bad day. I heard many people say that they felt surrounded by death, being reminded of fatalities on any and every platform. To be surrounded by death and unable to participate in death rituals can result in ambiguous loss, therefore complicating the grief process. Noticing the loose ends with no string in sight and closure never coming. The increased fear and uncertainty were unmeasurable. A client who I was working with was suffering from severe anxiety around getting the virus. In a particularly elevated session, she said, "healthy people are dropping dead." Those words were haunting. She wasn't wrong; this was happening all around the world, and if you didn't know someone personally, the media took care of having you feel like you did.

It is a challenge to articulate all the losses because it was like a car pileup that you can't stop from happening and you also can't look away from. And afterward being left with *how did this happen; when will this be over; I thought I was so careful.* For many of us, the loss of connection, physical touch, and interaction with others were profound. Bargaining with ourselves in efforts to find an answer to knowing if it is worth seeing loved ones six feet apart

---

[1] Haley, "Types of Grief: Yes, there's more than one."
[2] Williams, "Cumulative Grief aka Grief Overload."

while fighting the urge to embrace. Loneliness and cabin fever on the rise as the world waited for a vaccine. Our grief had nowhere to go because we had nowhere to go.

Finding and having connections with others is imperative to humans, and at the most foundational level, we want to be understood. 2020 only validated that social interaction and interpersonal connection are paramount. The predictability of life became lost for many, whether this was seen in job layoffs, postponed or canceled graduations, schools closing, or simply being able to afford everyday necessities. Feeling one unfair thing on top of another, not knowing how to cope with any of it, and due to the distance apart, whether it be six feet or across the globe, lots of us felt unable to grieve in the way we wanted, close to our loved ones. Holding both the unknown of our personal future as well as the unknown of the way our community, country, or the world was going to function is surely a lot to carry. It wasn't until we lost it that we may have realized how much our mental and physical stability relied on predictability. I saw a lot of clients who would report sadness but didn't know why. Though impartial to the pandemic, I would ask about changes in routines, vacations, roles, etc., and more than not, clients would report that there was a loss or change. This is frequently difficult to identify or even to validate within ourselves, as it falls under abstract loss. Abstract loss, grieving non-tangible or perceived things, was in abundance, and it wasn't always seen as something to grieve. To be more intuitive to this, an interesting exercise to do with yourself when you are feeling sad or down is asking yourself, *have I experienced a loss that I haven't yet grieved?*

It can be difficult to know what action to take with abstract loss. One of the most crucial things we can do for ourselves is to notice the feelings we are having and validate them. Abstract loss can be just as painful as physical loss, and therefore, the grieving experience is just as important. Though a challenge, there is power in articulating and naming what we have lost. Once we do this, we can start the process of learning what we need to do to attend to the void and feel like ourselves again. Identifying what the loss is and what it meant to us allows us to replace it in a way that is meaningful. It allows us to fill our cup restoratively rather than turning to drugs, alcohol, food, work, or other addictive behaviors.

With all the traumatic events that have occurred in the past year, it has been tough for some people to not feel trapped in the guilt cycle. The "other people have it worse"-like statement generally does not serve much purpose if it's being served with a side of guilt. I will let you in on a secret: This will always be true. Someone else *will* always have "it" worse, just as someone else *will* always have "it" better. So many of us get stuck trying to find our place on this line of comparison, now sprinkled with silver linings in the form of "at least." Reframing our thought pattern from something like "I shouldn't be upset. Other families have it worse because both partners lost their job and only my husband lost his. At least I still have my job" to "It has been so financially and emotionally hard since my husband lost his job, *and* I feel grateful that I have been able to keep my job." Reframing comparison when attached to shame is a grinding task, and we are often up against a lifetime of learned self-criticism. I assure you, though, there are very few things more freeing when you succeed in this.

Another historic sequence of events that 2020 forcibly called attention to was discrimination and racial injustice. Both discrimination and racial injustice have been persistent endurances, exceptionally emphasized in Black and Indigenous people of color (BIPOC) communities, that in recent times became amplified by white individuals and organizations. To comprehend the significance of this, acknowledging the intersectionality of identity is of value. Intersectionality describes the interconnectedness of social categorizations such as race, class, and gender. These then create multiple overlapping and interdependent systems of discrimination.[3] For example, I am thirty years old, cisgender, white, bisexual, middle-to-upper-class, Jewish, and female with pronouns she/her. As such, my views come from the lens of how I identify. I also identify with having white privilege. This is an unearned and unfair privilege in society that benefits me, whether it be financially,

---

[3] Boston, "What Is Intersectionality, and What Does It Have to Do with Me?"

politically, or socially, because I am white over BIPOC. As a white person, I was subtly, and sometimes blatantly, taught to not recognize white privilege.[4] This has led white people to express what is known as white fragility: feeling uncomfortable and defensive when white individuals are confronted by conversations or information about racial inequality.[5] In consideration of the lens that I see the world, I hope to redress by acknowledging that my experience and perspective are different from others.

Racial disparities have been historically prominent within BIPOC communities, and in 2020, they gained attention in a more mainstream way. Structural racism became an overdue focal point of conversation in communities and households. Structural racism refers to a system where "public policies, institutional practices, cultural representations, and other norms work in various, often reinforcing ways to perpetuate racial group inequity." It reflects in history where "whiteness" was allowed privilege, and "color" was a disadvantage.[6] In 2020, many Americans gathered in the growing Black Lives Matter movement through protests, education, and conversations. Created in July 2013 by Alicia Garza, Patrisse Cullors, and Opal Tometi, Black Lives Matter grew louder as Black people continued to be widely discriminated against and killed by police. The mission of Black Lives Matter, which is now a global movement, focuses on extinguishing white supremacy and in turn building power to stop violence against Black communities.[7] Granted that, by no means starting in 2020, it was a year where white Americans saw the increasing police brutality against BIPOC and were encouraged to address white fragility and check their privilege.

Experiences of grief and trauma were varied and became part of cumulative loss for many. The murder of George Floyd that was caught on video flooded media sites, asking viewers to both traumatize themselves and not turn away from gruesome realities. Doing therapy with clients during this time, I found it essential to create space for every client, especially BIPOC, to explore and process their feelings about these injustices and losses. A personal

---

[4] Lawrence et al., *Structural Racism and Community Building*, 15.
[5] Diangelo, "White Fragility."
[6] Lawrence et al., *Structural Racism and Community Building*, 11.
[7] Black Lives Matter Global Network Foundation Inc., "About."

opinion as a therapist is that I think that treatment plans are dumb. Sure, they can serve a purpose, but we all know that "life happens," in the broadest interpretation. When it does, that "plan" goes out the window. In the past year and some change, I often found myself steering away from the treatment plan and instead invited my clients to express what they were feeling and how they were coping when violence, death, and trauma were part of the everyday air. I asked about feelings of safety, sadness, and anger. If my client was part of the BIPOC community, I asked how it felt for them to have a white therapist during this time. In a more recent conversation with a client who self identifies as "a light-skinned Black girl who has struggled feeling like the other, not quite fitting in, and not quite being accepted but still feels it and still carries it," she states,

> You hope that if people saw it, then they would believe it, and it would change. But now to have it on video and for people to still deny it, rationalize it, even cheer it on, that kills my hope....Yes, it did elicit change at some level; there were protests. But then, we saw the disparity in how people were treated during them....I've been hiding from it and ducking it, but there's no hiding now....In a way, it's freeing....People think Tr--p created this....He didn't. He validated animosity. But it's been here. So, I feel so defeated and out of hope. I've learned to be small....I'm tired of the tax. I'm tired of paying the tax. It's a catch-22— you're hoping it wouldn't be there, but then how will people believe it if they don't see it?

A client of mine describes 2020 as "cavernous loss of self-expression," and in reflection of our 2021 therapy session, she starts to see this loss as what connects us to other people, even though it feels like it's what is keeping us apart. I was talking to my friend Mallory early into quarantine and ended up in a conversation that helped shape how I viewed the year. We had a Zoom dinner date, and she told me that a resident in her apartment complex held concerts on their balcony for the rest of the residents to enjoy through open windows and distant hellos. We spoke about all the changes that were happening with our jobs, businesses closing, and people isolating, never knowing what the next day was going to look like. I'm sure a lot of people were having these types of conversations. Mallory shared with me a phrase that her boss told the team in a recent meeting: "It won't be survival of the fittest; it's survival of the most adaptable." Though simple, I found this to be profound. It not only gave me a framework for understanding my own feelings, grief, and thoughts throughout the year, but it allowed me a new perspective on a broader grieving process. Now, over a year later, Mallory reflects with me that the only sliver of happiness she felt when stuck in a small studio apartment was the one window she could crack open to hear the music and see kids blowing bubbles out of their windows.

As a nation and planet, we were introduced to a threat unlike anything before. And as a nation and planet, we adapted in the ways we had to, while unfortunately and tragically losing people we love along the way. We continue to adapt and find resiliency among hate, and we continue to fight for racial justice. We learned that there are real-life superheroes living among us: grocery store employees, bus drivers, healthcare workers, mental healthcare workers, teachers, scientists, and many more. Whether it feels forced or welcomed, there is an opportunity to take an inventory of our life, priorities, and relationships. We were reminded time and time again that physical touch is pertinent, gratitude is powerful, and Black Lives Matter. I hope that the fragility of life is more prominent for us to see. How delicate human beings are under the right circumstances ... and tough as hell through others. And that we learn to find language that honors our experience of what happened in 2020, past "unprecedented." Because I for one felt like if I heard the word "unprecedented" one more time, I was going to lose it. A word used so often, I found that it lost its meaning. It was just the common adjective to describe tragedy or excuse things, even when the validity was unclear. It made me wonder if we were able to verbally express the profoundness and magnitude of the change and losses in our lives and the world. There seemed to be a change in how we used communication. What we said in our verbal communication, at times, felt more like a forced change to keep our livelihood and sanity. As the United States and other parts of the world continue to open back up, we have an opportunity to reflect. And if no one can fully articulate this true, worldwide "WTF" time in history that we have collectively experienced, we will be unified in that.

Part Two: Our Grief

Loss is universal.

Grief is individualistic and idiosyncratic.

Two years before the world quarantined, Mallory and I were in her kitchen having our own *what the fuck* moment. It was 2018, and she was still living in Austin, though she spent the summer in San Francisco for what appeared to be a promising opportunity for personal adventure and professional growth, helping build a startup with a couple she met through networking. I remember how excited Mallory was to go to the West Coast with a plan of moving there and the optimistic dream she had for the new company. Unfortunately, the dream was substantially oversold. The couple couldn't pay her initially, and as a tradeoff, they offered to let her live in their Victorian house, while she looked for a place to live when she moved west. Though hesitant, Mallory agreed. "By month three, I realized he had a coke addiction," Mallory says. "He was an ambitious, smart guy, but I finally decided that I can't stick around long enough to find out if he was going to pay me over doing drugs on a Tuesday." Not only was Mallory figuring out how to get out of this situation peacefully, but she also knew her grandma was dying back in Texas. She tells me, "While I listened to him snort it up at 4 a.m., I booked a flight home for that night. She died on my flight home, but I got to come home to be with my family during a hard time." Talk about culminative grief! When returning to Austin, Mallory grieved the death of her grandma, the disappointment and loss of a seemingly great job, and the future she pictured for herself living in the eclectically beautiful city of San Francisco. She was in a place of restless angst she had never been before, and there wasn't a map in sight. It was official: she was deeply lost. When she reflects on the experience, Mallory keeps a sense of humor: "They did a lot for me; I don't want to discredit that. But my lesson learned was don't trust anyone who quits their corporate job after they go to a Tony Robbins event."

I, too, felt similarly. As a new social worker who had never worked in the field passed grad school because traveling was a much-needed priority, I moved to Austin without a job—because why not? I needed one, though, because the sooner I started my clinical work, the sooner I could collect my hours for my clinical license. Higher license meant higher pay, and quite frankly, freedom to get out of the *systemically* undervalued, overworked, and underpaid daily grind. In May 2017, I started a full-time job working in housing services with the mentally ill homeless population. As one might guess, that shit was tough. I also worked part-time as a therapist for a pediatric group practice and a couple hours a month on a mobile crisis outreach team. When Mallory came back from San Francisco, I was overcooked and burnt to a crisp. I was pushing myself to get experience and to make enough money so I could afford rent, medical bills, and of course some Chinese food occasionally. But I was miserable. I met some amazing people while working these jobs, especially with the homeless population. I tried my best to find heart and appreciation for the work I was doing, like I saw in many of my tolerant coworkers. For work like this, you need passion, and I didn't have it. My attitude was getting worse and worse as I dramatically dreaded going to work. I was checked out. Even with this being the case, I still found my gratitude in the two fellow case workers that I unexpectedly became very close friends with soon after starting at the agency. Catherine and Shauna are the reasons I could sustain working that job and now remain distinctly treasured friends.

Returning to Mallory's kitchen, where both her and I were on the verge of clinical depression, with Jack Johnson playing in the background. Both of us felt stuck, hopeless, and genuinely scared that this was going to be our life because nothing was telling us differently. We were disappointed in where life had taken us but had no idea what the next play would be, in defeat thinking, *what the fuck do we do?* Mallory and I, together and separately, think about this time very often. In fact, without knowing it, we both use the same word to describe it: pivotal. It's because we served as each other's witness to the pain and discouragement for our present state and lacking confidence for the unknown future. We could have never known what was in store for each of us—and for Mallory, what was coming just two months later. What started as a part-time gig became an opportunity of a lifetime. Mallory first remotely joined as a Brand Creative Lead for a small consumer goods company. In about a year, she moved to Houston to start her new position with the company as Creative Director, building and leading a creative team of a hundred people.

I, on the other hand, had my own substantially oversold experience when I joined a new group therapy practice that led me to leave all three of my jobs and my benefits, only to be vastly financially and emotionally stung by the owners of the practice. Having to figure out a way to financially survive this period of increasing stress and decreasing mental health, I was hustling like I've never hustled before. Working up to six part-time jobs at a time and barely breaking even as I looked for a full-time therapy job that I wouldn't hate and I could trust. I was exhausted once again. In the midst of this hustle, I was applying to and writing TEDx Talks—until April 2, 2019, when I was welcomed to the TEDx stage. Speakers were given forty-one days to write, memorize, and prepare for May 12 in Colorado Springs. A journey with its own grief and pain yet was ultimately rewarding and an honor. Between May 2019 and May 2021, I became trained in Eye Movement Desensitization and Reprocessing, got hired as a therapist at a partial hospitalization level of care eating disorder facility where I learned and became a significantly better therapist, passed my clinical licensing exam, joined a new (*thriving*) group practice, started my own prosperous therapy practice, and signed a book deal. I also slept with the lead singer of my favorite band, who I had been in love with since I was a preteen—but now I'm just bragging.

Just like anyone else, there was loss, distress, and struggle sprinkled in that period of growth as well. Yet, I don't say that to minimize the awesomeness of my life because, honestly, it's beyond my wildest dreams. It's the perspective I choose to take, the ambition I worked to form an identity in, and the gratitude I carried every step of the way. I don't downplay my triumphs or my losses. Fuck that. I am fortunate of the opportunities that were presented to Mallory and me, and I am proud of the opportunities we made for ourselves. If only those women in that Jack Johnson music-filled kitchen could see us now. If only the twenty-four-year-old woman that only felt sorrow for the love that was taken could see me now. It took time, grit, and tears to get here. I suppose you could even call it a grief process. We made it through. Here we are on the other side.

***

Before taking on a new client, I will do a consultation call so I can assess for appropriate fit as well as give the client the same opportunity. Typically, a consultation call consists of finding out more about what brings the client to therapy, telling them about my style and therapeutic approach, and seeing if our schedules can match up. I describe myself the same way every time: "Foundationally, I am a relational therapist that empowers my clients. I call myself a validating challenger because I am a validation queen, and I'm also going to call you on your shit." When working on this book, it required me to reflect on how I operate as a therapist—why I practice in the way I do and what my "why" is so I can continue to embrace the gratitude that I feel for the work. I have really come to notice how essential the empowerment piece is to grief therapy. Grief can feel like a thief of identity, structure, and joy, replacing it with despair and unknowns. It isn't uncommon to isolate ourselves and pull away from support systems as we become incongruently content in the ditch where grief has spit us out. We feel alone, hopeless, and misunderstood and embrace the black-and-white narrative of superlatives: "I am never going to be happy again"; "I am totally alone, and no one will ever understand"; "Everyone is going to forget about me." Something any good supervisor or grad school will teach a future therapist is to meet the client "where they're at." This isn't always easy, but it is necessary because anything else is outside of the client's window of tolerance. I meet my clients in the ditch and help them set up camp for a bit and remind them not to get *too* content, because this isn't their new home. *NOT IN MY (therapeutic) HOUSE!*

Restoratively, over time, clients learn to climb out of the ditch on a ladder they made of coping tools. Shedding their chrysalis, they can radically accept that in the most beautiful of shades, their new world is gray, and they feel equipped to challenge the black-and-white thinking because they are empowered to do so. Coping skills bring structure, and empowerment brings new identity, sprinkled with resilience. My hope is that the people I work with find their own joy through the process of healing and learn that "living in the gray" means room for the stinging loss and the profound joy.

I hope that in this second part, you as the reader also feel empowered to have the courage to move through your grief. The best part is that you are not doing this alone, and I'll prove it to you. Without knowing you, I know you have gone through loss because the concept is too broad to have not, and let's face it ... the only prerequisite is to be alive. You read that right. I can vindicate that your pets and house plants also go through loss, but that will be in another book. Grief, on the other hand, is the response to loss and is unique to each person, while it paradoxically contains similar themes and experiences.

In 2019, I steadily became more curious about what I heard from clients I worked with when they spoke about their grieving experiences. Simultaneously, I started collecting research on experiences of grief from the broader public to identify common themes. In the pages following, I will uncover these themes from the research and from what I have seen as a grief therapist through statistics, stories, and quotes from therapy sessions and research responses. When we feel seen because we recognize another's experience as parallel to our own, we are then empowered to understand our own identity in the grieving process. I hope you see yourself in these pages.

Welcome to the gray. Hold on tight.

8

"People Tend to Listen

When They See Your Soul" [1]

"My grief is like the ocean, as it comes in waves—varying in size, location, reason. To make this brief, all within two years, I came to the gut-wrenching decision to break up with a boyfriend that was (is) struggling with an addiction to heroin, my brother completed suicide, and my mother developed very early-onset but aggressive Alzheimer's. There were large hits and crashes of grief, chaos, emotion, but as five years have passed, there are smaller, infrequent, unexplainable waves of grief that hit me (and sometimes have NOTHING to do with those three events). I do not believe that my grief will leave, and sometimes I have no idea what or

---

[1] Toro y Moy, *Freelance.*

why I am grieving, but it has never failed to teach me something."

Research participant, female, thirty, North Carolina

I started working with Anita* soon after she was diagnosed with breast cancer for the third time. Different from the other two times, this was stage four. The day before she started chemotherapy, we met for our weekly session and had a conversation about death. I asked if she was scared that she was going to die. Anita said, "Of course I am. I'm afraid of what I'm going to miss because I've lived a lot of life, but I'm not done yet." She talked about still wanting grandchildren. She asked me if I was afraid to die. I took a second to think, and I said no. I clarified to let her know that I was in no rush and had no desire to but that I felt as if when it was time, then what will be will be. I shared with her my perspective of putting fear on something that is at inevitable and in some ways totally out of my control. Unbeknownst to Anita, this made me think of the night in 2015, when I was sitting up in bed contemplating facing my own death. I told her that most of us who think about mortality probably hope for a painless death, and as painless as it can be for our loved ones. I feel grateful to have a perspective of dying that is encompassed with love. I often think of Drew's best friend Tyler's words at the funeral: "Though I do not wish it, I am no longer afraid of death." This simultaneously stayed with me as a beautiful reminder and as a haunting ghost. When I die, I know I have loved ones waiting for me, ready to welcome me to the realm with joy and open arms: my grandmother, my grandfather, Drew. A full-bodied love. It's that richness of what I have waiting for me that doesn't make me afraid to leave, nor does it make me depart sooner than I was meant to. Because like Anita, I also am not done here yet.

On a regular basis, I feel amazed that I get to have the job that I do. I have a mantra that I try my best to make the cornerstone of my day: *I am happy because I am grateful, and I am grateful because I am happy.* The amount of gratitude I have for the clients I work with is immeasurable. I am perpetually inspired by them and try to be a cheerleader for their progress. It is an incredible honor to work with people and help them through one of the most authentic and provoking times in their life. More than I had ever expected, as a grief therapist, I frequently am the person that hears certain experiences, thoughts, or feelings for the first time—things that nobody else knows. I would be lying if I said I didn't get validation from this, often strong enough to kick imposter syndrome's ass if I happened to be feeling any. This responsibility comes from a strong rapport and therapeutic alliance that I am grateful to hold with my clients, as I know their trust and vulnerability is a privilege to have. The other day, I was in session with a client, and she told me that over the weekend, during a challenging time, she heard me say words from a previous session inside her head. She explained that because she heard it from *someone else*, it had more meaning, and she was able to get through. The girl inside of me who is still eighteen and going to community college is awoken when someone tells me that they hear me in their head outside of session. The reality slaps like, *oh my God, I'm someone's therapist, and they remember what I say.* No presh.

From a combination of narratives from clients as well as my own self-awareness, I feel as though what has shaped me the most to be the therapist that I am is the lived experience of losing a significant loved one. Furthermore, I feel an unspoken responsibility to protect and care for my clients' experiences of grief. Of course, there are many other necessary qualifications to become a psychotherapist as well. But for many people who are grieving, it seems to make sense to work with a professional who not only understands and is knowledgeable about what you as a client might be going through from an educational background but also from having gone through a fiercely painful experience themselves. I choose to share my experience of losing Drew with many clients, as I see appropriate self-disclosure as an incredible rapport-building tool. I truly desire healing for them, as they show up for themselves and engage in a space that is safely created to share their story.

I started to notice that I aspired to broaden that safe space and understand more people's experience of grief. I had a hunger to further my knowledge about how people spoke about grief when offered a space and platform to do so. By providing this and evaluating results, I could not only develop new ways of understanding the clients I work with but also use findings to help educate the clients and audiences I speak to about grief that are backed up by research of real-life experience. Though trite, from a clinical perspective, I believe that knowledge is power. I use psychoeducation throughout the therapeutic process to help empower my clients and encourage self-compassion. Sharing my own research from a clinical yet relational stance strengthens the feeling of common experience, therefore decreasing feelings of loneliness. I had a goal and started my research development.

I read a solid amount of empirical research and peer-reviewed articles for the work I do. I find it to be helpful when I want a better understanding of something a client is going through or want to explore new methods or models to use with clients. I often remind myself that the data presented in the research I read are human beings and their experiences that, at times, have been diluted down to numbers and statistics. That is one of the reasons why I wanted to conduct qualitative research; frankly, it seemed less boring and allowed others to benefit from curious expression. I was less concerned about sharing statistics and wanted to share sentiment. Qualitative research has always felt like a soulful lifeforce rather than unadorned data. Qualitative researchers study in the natural habitat of the participants to captivate the human experience. The goal is to understand the social reality of the participants as clearly as possible, as if the researcher were the one living or feeling it; it becomes alive. The type of qualitative research approach I chose to do is called phenomenology. This is defined as the "study of the meaning of phenomena or the study of the particular." I was interested in the lived experience of the participants when it came to their history with grief. It is critical to note that in phenomenology, we look at the description of the event and the perspective of those who experienced it.[2]

---

[2] Tenny et al., "Qualitative Study."

Tell Me About Your Grief

I sent this prompt out into the world via Google Forms, primarily through email and social media. When the mood would strike me, I would also ask random people in the park, nightly Lyft or Uber drivers, and even Bumble dates. Using both convenience sampling, collection based on availability, and snowball sampling, collection by referrals from other participants, my goal was to collect and hopefully find similarities and patterns in the way we grieve.[3] I wanted to keep the prompt brief and rather vague so that there would be little direction to the participant on how to answer, while still generally knowing what I am asking them to talk about. I was eager to know how people would use a platform like this. Would they fill out the form in a matter-of-fact fashion, or would they spill their hearts? Would they see this as a healing platform and use the opportunity to share what may not have been shared with others ever before? I curiously wondered how many people would share non-death-related loss or if that kind of loss would even cross their minds when asked about grief.

I'm grateful to have had so many people who wanted to participate and share parts of their heart and story during some of the most heartbreaking times in their lives. Over the years, I've read responses that have stuck with me and think about them quite often. There is one that was submitted very early on in May of 2019, just a week or so after sending out the first round of emails. It was from a forty-two-year-old woman in Texas who describes her grief as waves in a beautiful poetic description that I believe will put words to many people's experience of grief. I remember the tears tickling my face as I swallowed her words up from off the page. Here is how she captures it:

My grief can best be expressed as ocean waves. Sometimes, it is powerful, engulfing, overwhelming, and consuming. Sometimes, it hits hard, and fast, and painfully, like a

---

[3] Tenny et al., "Qualitative Study."

sharp gut punch, reminding me that there is a
distinct absence of someone or something. It
is sudden, rapid, and even though I see it
coming, there's no amount of holding my breath
sometimes that can help me weather the waves.
I fall, perish for a moment, wonder if I will
surface again, wonder if I can keep holding my
breath for long enough for this, too, to pass.
In those times, it is inevitable that I come
out feeling a bit battered, like eating sand
from the ocean floor after a surfing wipeout.
No matter the amount of preparation or warning
or foresight, the grief can be all-consuming
and knock me flat where I can lapse into a
deep sadness, or anger, or turn on myself
because the pain of the loss is so great. When
the tides subside, and the waves calm to
swells, my grief becomes this pervasive, low-
grade infusion of sadness and absence. In
those moments, I'm swept in and out with the
ebb and flow of gentle but poignant grief,
reminded that I can and will move on, and I
will survive this one more day, but that
nothing will ever be the same, and that marks
an intense sadness coupled with an intense
love and intense longing, but subtle, like it
is interwoven into my soul, a dull ache.
Breathing feels just a bit more heavy and
effortful, like the weight of the world has
gently bore down on my being. Grief can be the
purest of emotions because it is a time when
I can just miss someone without also having to
be perky and positive, or angry and
frustrated, or anxious and nervous. I can just

grieve, honor the loss, be with the loss, invade the space of the loss, and explore it and own it and become it for just a moment, evoke the memories of what no longer exists. Like crumbs of sand, the outlines of tides shrinking back into the abyss of the ocean, and the ever-predictable yet unpredictable balance and flow of the waves, so is my grief. I should say that I love the ocean, as crazy as the waves can be. I love and embrace my capacity for grief. I have become my grief in that I can access this part of my soul that has loved and felt deeply, rejoiced and challenged myself beyond what was possible, dived into the wreckage of another being, and loved them with my whole heart because of the wreckage and the tatters. Knowing that I will never regret a moment with them despite how painful it can be to grieve their loss. I'm grateful to even have losses to grieve because that means I loved well and hard and thoroughly and madly. Grief can be sad, but it is also a triumph; it is also a delicious slice of something wonderful that existed and perhaps I had a part in creating. Just because it isn't physically here does not mean it is gone, but I would do anything, just anything, for a moment where I could physically hold her again, touch her again, talk with her again, take a step away from the ache and into the joyful rapture of being in her presence again instead of just being in her cosmos and her soul. That feeling sometimes, like the painful and powerful waves crashing, marks the difference from just missing her to wishing she was here again. The latter is grief to me. Sometimes, I'm wishing that the grief would subside, but other times, I almost latch onto it, because it gets me believing in something beyond this life, something important and meaningful, something good and kind and beautiful, something wistful and painful, something haunting and infusing into your soul. Because I do feel an intense and real sadness when I think of her. My entire being aches and longs and cries and wishes for her. Then I remember if I can still feel her loss, and grieve her physical absence, then she must still be here. And that thought, once I play the tape through, counterbalances the sadness with comfort and joy and peace. And then I jump back on the surfboard and paddle out to the waves to meet my grief again, allow it to envelop my core and my being, become one with her again, and never know where I begin, and the universe ends. Grief is what makes me feel real and alive, and meaningful, and purposeful, because it just means that I get to remember her and recreate her and refine her. Grief means she's never really gone because you remember her, and you feel her, and you know her. But grief also means that at one point, she left.

9

Dark Blue

"**M**y grief sneaks up on me and sometimes defines me. I was married happily for six years. I got separated at seven years and divorced just after eight years. I've been divorced for one and a half years, and I feel like my heart will never recover. I miss the person I was when I was married and happy. I miss the person I was in a partnership. I feel like I'll never attain the happiness I once had and kick myself for letting it go. But the grief sneaks up on me. I go into Whole Foods, and the smell of fresh groceries reminds me of all the meals made together. I avoid cooking bacon because the smell reminds me of the countless Sunday mornings spent together eating breakfast, enjoying each other. My grief feels like it's getting bigger at times as time goes on. I'm no longer paralyzed by it now. It doesn't pull me down like it used to, but it does crash on me like waves. I'll go weeks without thinking of my divorce, and then it will strike me so hard and cruelly. And I feel alone in my grief. No one else was a part of this relationship—

except my ex. But then, I'll never know his grief. So, I feel alone in it, and I feel like I have to hide it because I made a choice to be in this state. I left the marriage. And my grief is so much about my identity. I am divorced now. I am a divorcee, and the word hurts me. Because it says so much about me and so little. And all of it hurts. People say that the pain will fade in time, but I just don't know if it will. I feel like grief is hiding around every corner, and I can't escape it. And I'm alone just waiting for the next wave."

Research participant, female, thirty-five, Texas

The word *grief* falls somewhere between a trigger word that brings a somatic discomfort and an urge to change the channel. I commonly hear the explanation for not talking about grief—either as the griever or the supporter—is because we don't want to upset the other person. What do we even say? We don't know if it's our place; better to stay on the side of caution and not bring it up. *Can you hear my eye roll?* Caution for whom? Are we the ones that don't want to be uncomfortable, so we table the topic and find something else? Using the excuse of not wanting to upset the other? Are we uncomfortable with the expressed emotion that is frequently riding shotgun with loss? As we have gotten more awkward and intolerable with grief and death, the more we try to manage it rather than appreciate it as a natural experience. What's commonly heard by many people are clichés and empty banter that usually invalidate and push away any actual possibility of connection to a person who is in pain. What we say might not always be what the griever will hear. For instance, take these:

Life doesn't give you anything you can't handle = *I sure don't know how to handle this right now. Hope they figure it out.*
They would want you to be happy = *Your sadness makes me uneasy and kind of feels like a bummer.*

They're in a better place = *Yes, you're upset, but you should really be happy for them.*

Everything happens for a reason = *I don't know why this happened.*

Just look toward the future = *Please hurry up.*

The experience of grief is widespread, though the language of grief is spoken by far and few between. Just like any other language, we aren't born with the ability, and it needs to be taught, modeled, and practiced. I believe that, therefore, a very high number of people are uncomfortable with grief, and more candidly, mental health. We're illiterate. We don't know the "right" things to say. We are told that vulnerability isn't a desirable feeling, and it might have directly or indirectly been modeled from a young age that it isn't appropriate to share intense "negative" emotion because other people don't want to hear it, and it's not their business. I found it so interesting that some participants of the *voluntary* research added language to their responses, supporting this impression of not wanting to be a nuisance.

This has probably come off as a crazed, grief-filled rant.

To make this brief....

Gracious, that's enough for now!

Anyway, I'm going to start rambling, so I will end it there.

Sorry for this being so long!

This probably sounds like no big deal....

We're vulnerable. Even when we are willingly sharing our grief, there is maybe just a little, itty bitty, tiny, slightly possible part of us that isn't completely sold on it being safe, so we add the disclaimer. This language is seen in other ways too. We might feel worried about how others will respond to the loss, so we downplay the message, delicately doing our best to not upset the other person. I've also seen this done in efforts to protect ourselves because we might not know how we will react hearing ourselves use truthful language or react to the reaction of the person we are speaking with. I saw an example of this in a response from the research:

> "When I'm asked or the topic comes up in conversation, I'm in awe of how many women experience this, but then there's times you feel like slapping a bitch because she says, 'I can carry a baby for you. You know I got two.' The insensitivity on this subject amazes me, and sometimes, I wonder if people know that they're being insensitive."
>
> *Research participant, female, thirty-one, Maryland*

We might respond to others when they comment or condole a loss we have had with a response such as "It was a long time ago; it's okay; they went peacefully." Though this all might be true, it doesn't make the grief necessarily easier to deal with. One perspective of why it's so challenging to share our loss with others is because when we attempt to lean on others, it can end up as us comforting them, convincing them that we will be just fine. This persists a cycle of isolation as we distance ourselves because it's hard to continue to do this, causing us to limit the expression of our grief.

"Jeffrey's suicide shaped me, for the good and the bad. This event uprooted my life and sent me spiraling into young adulthood at the age of 10. Over the course of the next few months, people offered me empty, placating condolences, trite sentiments about how loss gets easier over time, how things will "work out," how Jeffrey was in a happier place now, no longer in any pain or suffering. My grief, my pain made people uncomfortable, and it was almost palpable. Instead of them consoling me, I found it was me who tried to console others. I learned how to shove down my feelings, putting them someplace deep inside of me that felt inaccessible."

Research participant, female, thirty-one, Baltimore

In a recent session together, my client Zayne* shares how he feels about talking about the effects and outcomes of his grief, even to his support network. Zayne states that it makes him feel like he is victimizing himself, fearing being isolated by his friends. The discomfort he experiences with verbalizing his feelings about the death of his mother in 2019 leads him to withdraw and feel distance between him and friends. Feeling pressure to grieve in a certain way is often reported in the work I do. It can be challenging when our grief doesn't show up for us in a way that meets internal or external expectations. We might feel rushed or misunderstood, leading the language around the loss to be even more difficult. Knowing that this feels true for many people, I am here to tell you that you are allowed to make a big deal about things you care about, and you deserve to have a safe place to learn the language of grief.

Gia*, who is in her late thirties, has been coming for therapy with me for a little over year. We started just about two weeks after the sudden death of her husband during a routine surgery. Gia has expressed deep sorrow in our sessions, describing somatically painful feelings as well as the desire and action of pushing away feelings by numbing out. In a more recent session, a little before the one-year anniversary of her husband's passing, Gia talks about the acceptance of her grief, giving herself *permission* for expression.

"If I'm having a bad day, it's okay to tell [my staff] I'm having a bad day....If they aren't comfortable with me crying, then they shouldn't ask about my day. I don't want to be afraid of sharing [my grief]....The brave face isn't real; I'm not going to not cry in front of someone."

Gia isn't alone in recognizing that "the brave face" shown to others is not always what or how we are feeling. A response from the research shares:

"During the next few days, I experienced an unstable emotional state: smiling at work, crying at home. Pretending that everything was okay with a big smile on my face and confidence. But it was not. Once alone at home, once everyone couldn't see me, I was just crying and feeling miserable."

Research participant, feminine, Québec

Gia has done a stunning job of embracing the gray and using her "and." She has learned that grief isn't linear, and though she experiences days of acceptance, the urge to change the subject or even flirt with denial is not unfamiliar: "If I'm having a good day, I don't want to ruin it by talking about grief." I normalize this.

Because if you think about it, especially with some added compassion, it completely makes sense.

We as a species don't do a good job tolerating loss or discomfort of any kind, and that includes change. Most people's automatic reaction is to look away, avoid, or distract. I tend to use normalization to explain this: "Of course, your reaction is to turn away. It doesn't feel good! Most of us will avoid things that hurt. *That's logical.*" Many of us even cross our fingers and hope that the grief will fade away over time if we pretend it isn't there. But as you might have guessed by now, it's important to face that shit—otherwise, she is here to stay in the most creative of places. Á la hide and seek. There is no doubt that grief is challenging, but it's not always overpowering. Being such an individualistic experience, it will often cause our raft to encounter some rapids, but rarely are they class six. How do we know we have "completed" the grief cycle, though? Trick question with an annoying answer: everyone grieves differently, so there isn't an answer, not a definitive one, at least.

A common theme that is expressed in grief theories and personal experiences is that healing takes time—and often is in no rush. When we have cumulative grief, a.k.a. loss on top of loss, we often feel overwhelmed and therefore can't give the loss the appropriate attention. In conclusion, we welcome the fan-favorite defense mechanism of avoidance. In the therapist role, I am frequently asked if there is a difference between avoidance and distraction. Here's the scoop: avoidance is boundless and generally grounded in discomfort or fear. We might not be aware we are doing it, as it is a passive coping mechanism. While bringing regulation and soothing, it doesn't last and will increase the anxiety and avoidance cycle. Distraction is a skill where we intentionally step away from the stressor temporarily until we are back in our window of tolerance and feel more regulated. By using distractions, we have all intentions of coming back to the stressor when we can engage in an effective way.[1] When we aren't judgmental, we can see that both avoidance and distraction serve a purpose. I normalize both by sharing that through using these ways to cope, we can keep functioning and maintain responsibilities or simply take a break

---

[1] DeRose, "Avoidance Versus Distraction: Which One Are You Doing?"

from feeling such intense emotion, because who likes to feel bad? With avoidance, especially when we start to feel overwhelmed by anxiety or grief, it is important to remember to make a deliberate effort to face the loss.

It's common to see patterns in avoidance habits, and it might be hard to identify if you're the one avoiding. Here's some help:

- Postponing: Delaying expressing grief in the hope that it will go away. Think of when we push a feeling or task away with the belief that it will grow feet and leave us alone. When we postpone, we often need help understanding that when we express our grief and pain, we can heal.

- Replacing: Taking emotions that we felt in the relationship for the person or thing that we lost and reinvesting the emotions prematurely to another relationship. Think of experiencing a breakup and getting into another relationship quickly afterwards. It is difficult to confront loss but necessary to be fully present as we move forward.

- Minimizing: Being aware that we are grieving and having emotions we aren't comfortable with, so we dilute them— trying to get through the grief quickly. This is similar to intellectualization by putting words in place of demonstrating emotion.

- Displacing: Taking the expression of grief from what we lost and instead attaching the feelings associated with it to something less threatening. This can look a variety of ways, from submissive to pushy to aggressive.

- Somaticizing: Transforming the feelings of grief into physical symptoms. Think of feeling anxiety and noticing you have a stomachache. This also has a wide range, from simple complaints to serious and even patterns matching a diagnosis. Another way this may be seen is by getting our emotional needs met through physical symptoms if it is seen as more acceptable in our environment.

Noam Shpancer, Ph.D. writes an article exploring the three principles between surviving and thriving. He says, "Emotions are good consultants but lousy CEOs. Consider their input but don't let them take charge."[2] It's solid advice, and the concept supports the dialectical gray. It is so important to learn to validate our emotions while also recognizing that there are skills to help us emotionally regulate, particularly in the world of DBT. The crux of the grief process usually occurs rather quickly. We see this in the ability to "continue" in whatever way that may mean for the individual. For example, we lose our job and a few days later start looking for new ones. We went through a certain process to allow ourselves to get to the point that we were ready to look for new jobs. That being said, "quickly" is subjective to the individual. I see this even in small ways with clients, people in my life, or even with myself: continuing to take care of children, going back to work, hanging out with friends, *and* still experiencing significant grief. You don't get over it; you learn to live with it.

I believe that when we can wake up every day and face our grief and start talking about it, it creates a ripple effect, and others feel safer to talk about it. Growing up on the East Coast, I relate this to something that is commonly done there: jaywalking. Now living in Austin, I noticed that a lot of people don't do this, probably because it's illegal and potentially very dangerous. Yet, it's something I got very used to doing when I was living in Baltimore and now a hard habit to break. When I don't see any cars coming but don't have the right of way, I am typically the person who starts walking across, and from my experience, others follow. As if they were waiting for someone to do it first. Relating this back to grief, when we take the first step and share our feelings and what we are going through, it can give our neighbor the confidence to also engage. They might just be waiting for the invitation to get to the other side.

---

[2] Shpancer, "Laws of Emotional Mastery."

"My grief has been rough and lonely. It's a
constant and spontaneous pop-up in my daily
life that I haven't quite learned to manage.
My grief has also been life-changing. It's
difficult to be around people since the few
times I've been open about my grief, they
are immediately uncomfortable."

*Research participant, female, twenty-six,
California*

The feeling of loneliness is one of the most common
proclamations I hear among anyone I speak to about the subject of
grief. This doesn't feel surprising, though it is strange to me. This
goes way past grief as well because for something that is felt by so
many people, it's hard to find "the cure." Even when we might know
we have support and are surrounded by people who love and care
about us, the only thing that might be felt is the emotional and
physical void. This emptiness is what we often refer to when we are
talking about feeling alone. This experience is normal, and grief can
really take the wind out of us, again and again. My client Gia would
tell me this all the time. Every morning when she wakes up, she is
missing a husband. The physical and emotional void is the first thing
she starts her day with, every day. The experience of loneliness
exists when there are multiple people grieving the same person as
well. While we can certainly empathize with the grief of another,
just as they can with ours, these are uniquely two different
experiences. Gia spoke about this often, on how she could never
understand the feeling of her husband's family losing a child or a
brother, yet they couldn't identify with her in losing a spouse. The
person she lived with, slept next to, quarantined with, and was part
of her daily life was quite suddenly gone. Gia has a good support
system, filled with family and friends to help her navigate the best
they can, though she is not the only one if she feels like this isn't
enough, and she is sailing alone.

The similarity of a loss can be viewed from a dialectic stance as well. While some may not find comfort in the presence of others who are grieving the same loss, there are many examples of how grief brings people together. This is the purpose of support groups: bringing those with a common history or understanding together to fight off the loneliness. Grief has the ability to connect us, and vulnerability, sharing, and emotions are contagious. I have seen this firsthand on many occasions, though most recently in a grief support group I created for those who have lost a loved one. Like the clients I see in individual therapy, I also feel there is an appreciation for a facilitator of the support group for grief that has had a battle with it themselves. I'll tell the people I work with, "I know what it's like to be stuck inside the worst moment of your life." Because time and time again, the following statement is defended:

It doesn't take someone special to understand that you are going through pain.

But unless you get it, you don't get it.

Finding comradery, finding community, that's how we manage. Even as I was writing, formatting, and collecting data and thoughts for this book, I was connected back to people who I had lost touch with over the years that helped me through my grief. It awoke a familiar gratitude that helped me through times of suffering. I felt lucky enough to witness similar gratitude in the first round of the grief support group. Coming to the group for the first time, the only thing they knew about each other was that they each had lost a loved one. But week after week, a similar narrative became familiar to everyone's ears. The participants thought that they were alone in what they were feeling. Some people called themselves crazy for the emotions that were swallowing them whole or the rituals they would do to get through another day of grief. Almost every time, the person succeeding them would say, "I feel the same way"; "I do that too"; "I didn't know other people experienced that." It seemed that for the first time for some people, they got to be around others who were in a similar spot in their grief journey, and it presented a safe space to be tenderly seen. The relation to each other becomes a common language, and there isn't a need to explain yourself. The environment is different because we can take in and recognize the unspoken pain. For example, two individuals in the group who were the same age recently experienced the death of a parent. They had individually shared that they didn't know anyone else that had lost a parent at a young age. It was beautiful to see the appreciation they felt for the other person because they knew someone else shared their sadness.

"Finding the similarities makes you feel normal when you feel alone."
Grief group participant

"It's nice to talk to someone who understands the strangeness of grief....not only verbalize but visualize what I'm feeling. I want the person I'm speaking to to feel it, to get what I say."
Grief group participant

Speaking from experience, I don't think we ever expect or can prepare ourselves for the loneliness, especially because it may not hit us initially when we first go through the loss. In Judaism, there is customary practice that you bring food to the mourning. When there is a death, often we sit Shiva and are surrounded by members of the Jewish community as well as individuals that make up our support network outside of the Jewish community. But you don't have to be Jewish to notice it's generally accepted that after a loss, especially a death, there are higher numbers of people reaching out. People offering and being supportive, physically engaging with the mourner, and understandably recognizing the loss. Though, just like everything else, the intensity of it rarely lasts.

"Another part of the loss is that everything goes on. Life goes on. You feel like the world should just stand still for a while when someone leaves us. People should stop

going to work, stop being happy, etc. It
feels like the person who is gone didn't
matter since everyone just keeps going about
their business."

*Research participant, female, forty-two,
Maryland*

Acknowledging again that society doesn't cope well with grief or loss only reinforces the cycle of loneliness. Refusing to be mindful that pain, illness, death, and grief are part of life, we can irrationally believe that it won't happen to us or the people we care about. But think again! Having this perspective makes us unsuspecting and ill-prepared to deal with the grief and the feeling of being alone, even though it is a remarkably lonely affair. A large part of feeling lonely during this time relates back to the previous research response. Many people feel that no matter how many people are around, truly doing all they can to support us during the time of grief, our life has taken a pause. It really can feel like you are stuck in the worst moment of your life. So, even when you have loved ones coming to your home to support you, when they leave to go back to theirs, they continue with life. For those grieving, we are back alone in our life that came to a brutal halt.

Audree* was referred to me by a colleague who thought that we would be a great fit together, and I would be able to give her the support that she needed for the challenges life had thrown her way. Within the span of five years, she has undergone multiple surgeries, including a brain tumor removal, left a longer-than-a-decade relationship, and endured the separate deaths of her mother, father, and sister. Audree was struggling with coping mechanisms in dealing with all of this, to which I often think, *who wouldn't?* We had our work cut out for us. Most of our sessions consist of her verbal processing and me doing Socratic questioning and active listening. We both have learned how important it is to verbally express her process so she can get to a place of understanding, flexibility, and self-compassion. I find this to be true for a lot of clients. When they are given the space, especially to process out loud, they find the way on their own. This is increasingly more powerful than me giving them the lightbulb moment. If you want to help someone through grief, feel free to do what I do in a session. I listen. People have very few spaces to be heard and *feel heard.* Know that there is a power in silence. When people have space and aren't afraid of ending a sentence because they fear that the other person is preying on the capture of the spotlight, real magic can happen. When people have uninterrupted space where they feel heard, they are more inclined to be curious and explore. In fact, not long ago, Audree said something that I was utterly taken aback by:

The closer I am to the person [I lost], the more distant I am from everyone else around.

First, having to pause and digest her insightful words, with my hand over my heart, I told her I was emotional. She responded telling me she was, too, as I saw her wiping a tear from her eye.

The experience of grieving multiple individuals as well as non-death loss can be an exhausting and confusing ride. When we are experiencing cumulative loss, it's important to remember that the grief we go through is unique and individualized to each person we lost and each loss we endure. Unfortunately, we can't bunch them together and think we will heal them as one. Remember that bereavement looks different for everyone, and it also takes into account the role of the deceased and the relational history between the individuals.

"I got angry as I grieved my mother and brother simultaneously because I felt so alone in my sadness. It's weird because I feel like my grief kind of went away until the last year or two, and now I think about my mom and brother all the time. I just wonder 'what if' and why it happened. I feel

```
       like I was cheated out of two
               relationships."
```

Research participant, female, thirty-eight,
Texas

     I believe that a benefit that occurred for Audree as she has gone through therapy has been that there are two minds working together to put the pieces together and that each has a different perspective. There was a session where Audree seemed to feel especially surprised by this, as we were exploring negative cognitions of a coping mechanism she used: "You didn't attack the symptoms. You cut through the bullshit and reframed the whole process. You focused on the broader thought process and have given me another angle to look at this from."

     I think a large reason why grief is often so arduous and painful is that it takes so much from us and steals our love and our hope. We love the people who die, the relationships that end, the job that we lost. Our connection to these things creates a world of hope that became part of a narrative we planned on seeing through. So much of our own identity is in the way we love, and in parallel, the way we grieve. Be as that may, are we oblivious to this? If we grieve in the way we loved, I wonder how that would change our experience. How would it change the relationship we have with even the word *grief*? If we entered grief in a similar way we enter love, what would that be like? And are they just one and the same?

     Loss of identity is a particular type of loneliness. Not even having all of yourself for familiar comfort can feel outlandish. We can feel grief to anything that is a part of our identity. In addition, when we feel grief, it cuts the essence of our identity. So, here we are, grieving the loss of something or someone and feeling like part of ourselves is also gone. We *then* might grieve that additional loss of some part of ourselves or our identity. This can become a bit of a mindfuck. The jarring reality is that, for most, our identity goes through more of a shift than a total disappearance. It's important to validate ourselves in this because by remembering the identity we had, we often will yearn to get it back in some way. We could potentially get close, but we won't ever have it back to the exact way we were before the loss. Continuing a connection, especially to a loved one who has passed, as well as the person who we used to be, can be very beneficial for our healing.

Loss of physical, spiritual, financial, social, or professional identities can also occur. I saw this impact with Malcolm*, a client of mine in his thirties who had suffered a traumatic spinal cord injury resulting in paraplegia. Instantly, his identity shifted in a major way as well as how he interacted with the world. Grieving the loss of the independence he once had and continuing to accept the level of independence he has now, Malcolm's grief around social and physical identities has taken a lot of space in our sessions. Interpersonal interactions were often filled with resentment, intolerance, and anger when he perceived someone "feeling bad for the cripple." Dating seemed significantly more challenging, as Malcolm would feel that women would dismiss him due to being in a wheelchair. In many ways, I thought that the deep layers of grief had given Malcolm an untrusting view of the world and the people living in it. I would often wonder out loud if he might be projecting in certain scenarios, such as someone running to hold the door open for him, where he would become angry and spiteful. Projection is protection. When we are in deep grief, it reasonably feels important to protect ourselves. However, the ways that we might try to protect ourselves often make us feel more isolated. Recently, Malcolm has opened to the idea of actively looking for ways to meet others and expand his interpersonal relationships. I see this as an effort to challenge the anger and help himself through his grief by expanding his relationships and engagement to strengthen his new identity.

It is commonly seen to take on grief as our identity. I hear about this incredibly often in my clinical practice and received multiple responses from participants of the research. When we are engulfed in our grief, it ends up being what is yelling the loudest. The part of us that is missing can feel too monumental to not only be contained but also swallows up the rest of the pieces of our identity that make us who we are. This can represent a version of what is called prolonged or chronic grief, where reactions are extended and intense, and the griever is often incapacitated by emotion and impaired in long-term daily functioning.[3]

"I have lost my two children and an ex-husband from the opioid epidemic. The first daughter died in May 2012, the second in December 2014. I am not the same person anymore. It is difficult to find things that matter and to keep going. Part of me is missing. I have to carry this grief the rest of my life."

Research participant, female, sixty-five, Maryland

"The death of my grandmother has made me preoccupied with thoughts of death. It's made me obsesses over one day losing my own mother. It's made me obsess over my own eventual death. I feel guilty for still being so torn up over my grandma's death two years later. She was ninety-five. It was time, but I miss her every day."

Research participant, female, twenty-nine, Texas

---

[3] Haley, "Types of Grief: Yes, there's more than one."

Research was conducted by Harvard University psychological scientists Donald Robinaugh and Richard McNally on individuals who experienced the death of their partner. Findings concluded that when a partner has died, it can be extremely challenging to imagine a future without that person still in our lives, leading us to have a loss of identity and intense helplessness. However, it seems to be quite simple to imagine an unfeasible future with the person who has passed, which is the cognitive grounds of persistent yearning.[4]

"Grief for me is essentially like being a tall building into which a bomb has been precisely dropped. The exterior shell is intact, but all inside has been blasted. From the outside, many don't even notice that the building has blackened windows or cracks out of which smoke is seeping. Still standing, seems just fine—BUT I WAS NOT FINE, and those nearest me knew that and forced me to go to therapy."

Research participant, female, sixty-six, California

---

[4] Herbert, "Mourning and Memory: A Paradoxical Grief."

"I understand grief is a part of life, and it's important to honor their lives. But I also refuse to let it hold me back from living. I've unfortunately witnessed that happen to my mother on more than one occasion. I don't want someone's death to become my identity—it scares me."

Research participant, female, twenty-nine, Texas

After weeks of heart-rending sessions with Gia, punctually surrounding the one-year anniversary of her husband's death, we came to the end of another mournful yet hopeful session. Gia shared her frustration with work and what has been so stressful in her professional life. She noticed that for the first time in a long time, there was something else to be upset about. Grief had been so intense that it felt good for her to be upset about something that wasn't her husband's passing. Gia gave herself permission to be distressed about other things, and it felt relieving to her! She discovered new insight that there was more to her identity. Now feeling "new" emotions that she had felt before when her husband was alive. With a new self-assurance, she ended our session with, "I can do this. I can survive."

10

How Did You Survive?

" **L**oss is such a universal experience and feeling, and yet it often feels so alienating and isolating. Traumatic grief left my brain void in a lot of ways. Some memories are seared into my brain forever, those I wish I could forget, but mostly there are vast periods of time that I can't remember. I think my child brain knew it had to protect me even when others wouldn't. "

Research participant, female, thirty-one, Maryland

The day Drew died, and I arrived at his house, I ran in the door and tried to go up the stairs to his room, but a policeman caught me in his arms, and I wasn't allowed further. Days later, when I returned to the chaos-settled house, I walked up to Drew's bedroom and saw blood on the carpet. From then on, I have a very clear and vexatiously persistent "memory" of Drew dead on the floor in this place where the blood had now dried. What I am describing is a common occurrence that people report when grieving that involves having memories of an event or detail around the loss that they did not witness. The term "false memory" describes a wide range of

184 *Adding the E*

distorted recollections or memory errors scaling from mundane, such as remembering to mail a letter, to consequential, like completely fallacious reports of an event in one's life.[1] Stress increases the likelihood of misremembering or having false memory. Research around memory has found that individuals with PTSD were more likely to create false memories, supporting the thought that PTSD substantially interferes with thoughts and memories that are "thematically related" to the disturbing event.[2]

Another interesting discovery that was found by Robinaugh and McNally is an emotional paradox of memory involved in complicated grief: "Compared to those who were experiencing normal grief, those with complicated grief had clear defects of both memory and imagination. They were unable to recall specific events from the past, nor could they conjure up detailed future scenarios....This cognitive deficit was apparent only when the events did not include the deceased. When recalling past events with their partner—or projecting future events—these extreme mourners were no different than the normal controls."[3] Recalling those we lost can come in various forms through our senses. Through examining research and literature about this, as well as considering personal experience, smell seems to be the most connected to emotional memory. According to Jay A. Gottfried, a neuroscientist at Northwestern University, the sense of smell is "our most primal sense and has intimate and direct control over emotional and behavioral states" and is distinctly true for very meaningful memories. Gottfried continues, sharing that an apparently arbitrary trigger can trigger something in the memory of the person we lost. This portrays what is called phantosmia, or olfactory hallucinations, experienced when we detect a smell that is not actually there.[4] That said, hallucinations are not atypical grief reactions. I have experienced this quite often, smelling the scent of Drew or the scent of his clothes at random times. I become overwhelmed with a composition of warmth, love, and deep longing. Our minds are

---

[1] Bluck, Newman, and Lindsay, "False memories: What the hell are they for?," 1046.

[2] Otgaar et al., "What Drives False Memories in Psychopathology?"

[3] Herbert, "Mourning and Memory: A Paradoxical Grief."

[4] Myerson, "Opinion | the Smell of Loss."

known to be tricksters at times, and when we are hallucinating the smell of someone we lost, it can feel comforting to know our brain keeps this emotional connection.

As a grief and trauma therapist, the two are really partnered together. If a client comes to me for trauma therapy, I typically make the judgment call that we will also be doing grief work. When someone comes for grief counseling, through learning the individual's narrative and physical and emotional experience of grief, I can determine what trauma interventions will be appropriate. Trauma can be difficult to even notice, let alone know what to do about it, if you aren't familiar with the signs. Psychoeducation has become a core piece of my therapeutic practice. I believe that when we understand why things are happening, it is easier to tolerate kindness for ourselves and therefore move closer to healing. I saw this almost instantly with Tiana*, a client I was working with to process a sexual assault. They had immense guilt for "letting it happen" and not doing something to protect themselves or stop it from occurring. I provided some psychoeducation on the five autonomic defense responses chosen unconsciously by our animal brain: fight, flight, freeze, submit, and attach. I explained that our body's number one priority is to keep us alive. Therefore, our nervous system goes into survival mode when a threat is perceived by the body. Tiana was able to identify that during the assault, they froze. I shared that from my experience of working with individuals who have been sexually assaulted, the freeze response is the one that is experienced the most. I validated that this is a *primitive brain* response that they were unable to have any conscious control over and that their body was doing what it needed to do to protect itself.[5] The self-compassion and understanding Tiana was able to give themself was beautiful to watch.

Bessel van der Kolk, an author, educator, psychiatrist, and researcher, is one of the most celebrated leaders in the trauma world. His quote on the presentness of trauma, rather than the past, is essential understanding for trauma work:

---

[5] Wagner, "Member Insights: Polyvagal Theory in Practice."

In fact, the past is the past and the only thing that matters is what happens right now. And what is trauma is the residue that a past event leaves in your own sensory experiences in your body and it's not that event out there that becomes intolerable but the physical sensations with which you live that become intolerable and you will do anything to make them go away.[6]

Van der Kolk often references a critical nerve in our body that connects the brain with the body and was first identified by Charles Darwin, the vagus nerve. When we have a strong emotion, we experience it at the midline structure of the throat, larynx, heart, lungs, and gut. This is the core of the vagus nerve, hence getting *heart-wrenching* and *gut-wrenching* sensations.[7]

Take this participant's experience, for example:

On my last relational grieving, my way to sadness was brutal. I was not prepared, not at all. I didn't see coming these magic words: we need to talk. I remember that day at work where my heart did a roller coaster ride into my body. I even thought that I will spit it out on my desk. I was not able to focus anymore. The way at home was blurred; my brain was haunted by these words.

Feeling as though her heart was free roaming through her body, a feeling that you might also have experienced before, shows the vagus nerve definitely being activated. Her lack of focus also speaks to familiar responses when there is hyperarousal. The vagus nerve is a bidirectional nerve, meaning that there are "signals going from the brain into the body and from the body into the brain."[8] This is why, for example, when anxiety is elevated, and we have a rapid

---

[6] National Institute for the Clinical Application of Behavioral Medicine, "How to Work with the Traumatized Brain."

[7] National Institute for the Clinical Application of Behavioral Medicine, "How to Work with the Traumatized Brain."

[8] National Institute for the Clinical Application of Behavioral Medicine, "How to Work with the Traumatized Brain."

heartbeat and sweaty hands but then can vividly visualize our safe place, we become more regulated. If you can calm down your body, you send signals up into your brain to then calm your brain.

From experimenting with the vagus nerve, Dr. Stephen Porges created the Polyvagal Theory. This theory consists of a three-part nervous system: the dorsal vagal system, the sympathetic nervous system, and the ventral vagal system. The dorsal vagal system, which is part of the parasympathetic nervous system, is the oldest of the three.[9] If we look back to Tiana's defense response of freeze, this means that their dorsal vagal nerve reacted and immobilized the body. This nerve is responsible for the ability of the body to shut down when threatened. If Tiana's primitive brain were to respond with a fight-or-flight response, that would be because the sympathetic nervous system responded to the threat. The ventral vagal system, which is the newest and most evolved out of the three structures, is termed the "social engagement" system. This is responsible for helping you feel a calm connection to other people when you feel safe in your environment.[10] Part of my job as a therapist is helping my clients feel a sense of safety while in session and work towards a sense of safety outside of the therapy session by shifting into social engagement biology. Exercises focusing on the mind-body connection, grounding, or mindfulness are all helpful. Have you ever noticed that when doing meditations, there is sometimes coaching to hum on the exhale breath? This is a great way to center and calm your nervous system, as the vagus nerve moves through the inner ear and vocal cords.[11] Singing also helps get the job done, so belt it out, sis! When I use reflective and active listening in a session, this also enriches the therapeutic bond, making the environment a safe place.

When working with clients who are experiencing complex PTSD, I will frequently see this paired with dissociative symptoms or dissociative disorders. Referencing back to the quote from Bessel van der Kolk, the sensory experiences and physical sensations can

---

[9] Wagner, "Member Insights: Polyvagal Theory in Practice."

[10] Wagner, "Member Insights: Polyvagal Theory in Practice."

[11] Wagner, "Member Insights: Polyvagal Theory in Practice."

become intolerable, and the body will find a way to cope.[12] This is how I explain this to clients who experience forms of dissociation; the body is doing whatever it needs to cope and withstand what it is going through, even if that means a little vacation from reality. I'm reminded of a client of mine in her early twenties, Ramona*. For being so young, she had endured pronounced losses along with significant trauma. Ramona and I started working together soon after her little sister had passed away from an overdose, now coming to therapy to do eye movement desensitization and reprocessing (EMDR) after feeling like she wasn't getting to where she wanted to be with talk therapy. Ramona, plagued by cyclical trauma, showed physical and emotional dissociative symptoms, suicidal ideation, and feelings of intense shame and guilt. She and I worked hard on calming her nervous system and finding a window of tolerance that she had been missing. I found it helpful to change the language I used and modeled in session, from asking how she coped with a dysregulating, triggering, or traumatic event to *how did you survive?* In a recent session together, Ramona says words that I have never heard her say before: "I'm so happy I don't want to kill myself all the time....I don't remember the last time I was this consistently joyful....I feel lucky." I am proud to say that Ramona has embraced the gray; proving to herself she survived, her head is above water, and she is managing the waves.

Flashbacks are a unique symptom to the diagnosis of post-traumatic stress disorder. When in a flashback, the individual is in a dissociative state caused by intrusive reexperiencing of a traumatic event in present time.[13] We have a timekeeper in our brain, called the dorsolateral prefrontal cortex, located in the frontal lobe, and its main job is telling us, "This is now, and that was then." This is the reason why very traumatized people have flashbacks and not memories: this part of the brain is missing! Consequently, the traumatic event that happened twenty years ago feels like it is happening right now, and your brain is unable to send out the information that this is a past event. One of the earliest studies on

---

[12] National Institute for the Clinical Application of Behavioral Medicine, "How to Work with the Traumatized Brain."

[13] American Psychiatric Association, ed. "Trauma and Stressor Related Disorders." 171–180.

PTSD showed that when individuals start reliving their trauma, a lot of their brain goes offline, and what was in the past is now feeling very real in the present. Another area of the brain that goes offline is located in the frontal region behind the left eye, called Broca's area or the speech center. When one really goes into their own trauma, they become dumbfounded and sometimes quite literally a speechless person. This only reinforces how important it is to keep these parts of the brain online, starting in a therapy session and often having the client practice on their own. Breathing, tapping, feeling your body, or having grounding objects can help us stay mindfully focused on the present here-and-now. Therapists can often serve as an anchor for traumatized people and an affect regulator who keeps their body safe and makes it safe for the client to think about the past and not let the past hijack the present brain.[14]

What about the brain on grief? Studying how humans cope with loss and extreme life events, Dr. George Bonanno, Ph.D. is a professor of psychology at Columbia University Teachers College and head of the Loss, Trauma, and Emotion Lab. The brain is a predictive organ. When we are attached to someone or something, it becomes part of our identity, and our brain is more likely to predict interactions that include that certain someone or something, even when they/it are/is no longer around.[15] For example, after Drew died, I still carried him around in my mind; there was a mental representation of who he was. My brain needed to adjust to what it meant that I will never see Drew again, while at the same time not completely erasing him from memory. We often see this when we think, *he would think this is so funny* or *I just saw something he would love.* The mind is constantly resetting and being reminded of the painful loss.

Sadness plays an important role in the reset. Our attention is now refocused from the world around us, to the world within us, subsequently offering to start the mental reset. Sadness that we feel appears to slow the world down, and when that happens, it sharpens our cognitive capability. Bonanno points out that not only is pain

---

[14] National Institute for the Clinical Application of Behavioral Medicine, "How to Work with the Traumatized Brain."

[15] Estroff Marano, "At a Loss."

after loss useful, but many behaviors and customs related to death are purposed to amplify the genuinely difficult course of adjustment. It's common for people who are mourning the loss to come together to honor the deceased and support each other. Very often, this makes acceptance of our loved one's death closer to our reach, and it reinforces our social bonds even with the loss.[16]

A twenty-nine-year-old research participant from Houston shares an example of this in her response:

```
My mother has always been a "grief dweller,"
idolizing those passed even when they were
terrible people and treated her horribly.
Turning the event of death and funerals into
almost an identity of sorts. She also has
become very symbolic, tying every person
who has died to a symbol—a bunny, a redbird,
a bluebird—and then begins collections of
items with those symbols on them. I think
they help her process. Help her feel close
to that person. Maybe even honor them?
```

In brain imaging studies of people who are profoundly grieving, there is high activation of the desire part of the brain, the corpus striatum. This is a major component of the reward circuit. In fact, activation in the corpus striatum occurs even when an image of the person lost is not being looked at or while the individual is doing a task that asks for their attention. This shows evidence of interfering thoughts. When recovering from grief, bereaved individuals show the same brain signature in the corpus striatum when they think about the person lost. Brain activity is also seen in the dorsolateral prefrontal cortex, the region of the brain that is responsible for

---

[16] Estroff Marano, "At a Loss."

executive control over memory, attention networks, and orchestrating cognitive flexibility. It was found that this was true even when the individual was not thinking of the person they lost. This concludes that it doesn't mean that the individuals in the study don't think about the person they lost; they are just able to put the thoughts aside and shift their attention from the interfering thoughts.[17]

I tell my clients that in grief and loss, we react, not respond. Emotional intelligence goes out the window, and suddenly, we are in a no man's land that is filled with sinkholes that can be so overpowering that we don't have a choice but to react. Therapy is a place where the reactions are explored and processed. Therapists hear about the sleepless nights, the split from reality, and the anger that has nowhere to go. I find that when working with clients who are going through grief and the trauma associated with it, it is often helpful to be curious of the reactions and emotions that one is feeling and learn what's actually happening in the brain. I try my best to get what belongs to my clients back to their lives and help them find themselves again. Grief makes us question who we are, what our lives are, and what there is to live for. If you lost that, I'll help you find it.

---

[17] Estroff Marano, "At a Loss."

11

Watercolors

"Then, I started to be on my way to anger. I stopped crying, and I started to get angry. The masculine gender made me feel so angry that my motto started to be *fuck them all! Fuck all these bastards!* The only thing I wanted was to grab a heart and smash it. Despite my calm attitude, deep into me, it was a total war. I was well decided to build a heart-wall protection against anyone who wanted to get too close. The nice girl was gone; the angry me was on the way."

Research participant, feminine, Québec

Anger. We all know it, and most of us are rather good at it. It's generally an easy emotion to feel, as it's often the surface and expressive emotion for a deeper group of emotions that might take some work to get through. Anger in the grief process could represent our awareness to the new reality that not only do we not want to tolerate, but we also protest it. Our desire to protest the loss we have endured usually matches the intensity of the emotions felt. Rather than feeling the pain that is very much alive, the pain ricochets into an expression of anger. Who or what are we angry at, though? A smorgasbord of things to take our pick from. Evidence from the research shares:

Feeling alone

I lost my job and can't find another because of this pandemic

Legal drugs that kill people

No one else in my life must go through this

Having no one to blame it on

No support group for caregivers of ALS patients in their twenties

I had to watch her waste away

My grandma for not being there to see me graduate

The cancer

Other people still had their parents, and I didn't

Our anger can be aimed at just about anything and anyone, justified or not. This can include others in our lives, strangers, the world, God, and even the person who died. That's a tricky one, too, because again, we are served the message that when we have such intense feelings of love or desire for a person who passed away, it wouldn't make sense, or it's judged to have anger as well towards the person. Though sometimes, this is exactly what can be holding us back from moving forward or even lifting a weight from our shoulders. It is normal to be angry with the deceased or with the loss, and it is important to give yourself permission to feel the anger.

"I still feel angry that he had to die that way, and I still blame him for smoking cigarettes as long as he did. As stupid as I feel admitting that, and as irrational as I know that to be, part of me is still mad at him. He missed out on very important things in my life that he should have been there to share with me. My grief feels selfish, but when I'm honest with myself, anger is what I still feel. My mom and her sisters, all nurses who took care of other people's grandpas without a second thought, fell apart and unraveled at the seams. I didn't have space to experience all of my emotions while all of the strongest women in my life were temporarily "out of order" in the department they were most experienced in. The hospital staff treated him like he was old, sick, and crazy (like a job). But he wasn't just old, sick, and crazy; he was a person with really amazing life stories before he became a shell. He had a pulse, but there was little to no recognizable life in him. He wasn't himself anymore, but there were moments where he'd make a joke or comment that would remind me he's still in there."

Research participant, female, thirty-one, Maryland

It's always fun to remind my clients that I, too, am a human and struggle with things just as anyone else does. I might be their therapist, but when I grieve and experience high amounts of stress, I shut down, and I shut people out. I will run DBT skills through my head and do my best to use some but then decide that crying and losing my shit in that moment feels so much better. Duh! It's that immediately satisfying sweetness of relief that actually helps us feel more in control. And man, if that isn't the core of anger ... am I right?

We can want control over the same things we are angry at: the situation, a person, ourselves, our environment, our circumstances ... the list could go on. Leon Selzer, Ph.D. describes how Steven Stosny, Ph.D. identified symptomatic anger representing the pain of what Stosny calls our "core hurts. These key distressful emotions include feeling ignored, unimportant, accused, guilty, untrustworthy, devalued, rejected, powerless, unlovable—or even unfit for human contact (cf. John Bradshaw's 'shame-based identity')."[1]

"I was angry. I was full of seething rage. I kept channeling that fire and storing it in the dark places. My child body was not used to carrying so much pain and resentment. Jeffrey was supposed to be with us. Any higher power was not supposed to let this happen. My parents were supposed to take care of us. Everything felt like it spiraled out of control. I panicked. I quit playing the flute. I quit eating pizza. I quit eating all together for a while. I obsessively spent hours styling my hair and painting my nails. I started plucking my eyebrows to thin lines. Anything that I

---

[1] Selzer, "What your anger may be hiding."

could control because everything felt so completely and terribly out of my control."

Research participant, female, thirty-one, Maryland

Stosny also speaks about the hormones released when we are in an episode of anger. The brain produces the "analgesic-like norepinephrine when we're provoked, but it also produces the amphetamine-like hormone epinephrine, which enables us to experience a surge of energy throughout our body—the adrenaline rush that many of my clients have reported feeling during a sudden attack of anger." Selzer explains how paradoxically adaptive this is. When we are hit by some type of situation, person, or stimulant that makes us feel powerless, we respond to this by turning the feelings of helplessness into anger, which then elevates perceived control.[2] *This* is the satisfying, sweet relief. It makes sense why it is many people's go-to emotion when we are threatened, distressed, or under the right circumstances, slightly inconvenienced; we feel empowered and entitled to keep that power for as long as we can.

"I pressed the panic button one time when I needed help because he lost his mind and was covered in his own feces and physically wanted to clean up on his own....Normally two hundred pounds, [he] was a whole ninety-two pounds soaking wet, so he couldn't stand up on his own, let alone clean himself. It took forty-five minutes for someone to respond, and by then, I had lifted him up myself and cleaned everything. As a form of control, I kept a log of how long it took for anyone to respond to the panic button,

---

[2] Selzer, "What your anger may be hiding."

as if me keeping this log was going to hold
someone or some entity accountable for the
lack of reasonable response. I felt
helpless, and anywhere from annoyed to angry
with the nurses, with him, with the cancer."

*Research participant, female, thirty-one,
Maryland*

As mentioned before, anger is often the surface or expressed emotion for underlying causes. When we think about the range of emotions we can experience, it can be helpful to increase emotional intelligence by becoming aware of primary and secondary emotions. There are multiple perspectives on primary and secondary emotions. For example, Robert Plutchik, Ph.D. identified eight different primary emotions: anger, fear, sadness, disgust, surprise, anticipation, trust, and joy. Primary emotions are what we initially feel to external stimuli, and secondary emotions are the reactions we have about having the primary emotion.[3] We can also understand this from a flexible, individualized level, rather than definitively primary or secondary emotion. I find this to be truer, especially with anger. When I am working with a client that is either reporting anger in the moment or reflects on an anger episode outside of session, I will ask, "What is the foundational (primary) emotion?" If they can't identify it, another path of exploring this would be to ask them, "What happened directly before you felt anger?" For example, experiencing infidelity can be an intense grief process. Gemma* was a client of mine who had recently found out about her husband's affair while she was pregnant with her third child. She has intense anger that would fill the therapy room, which I felt was important for her to let out. After a couple of sessions, I explored the purpose of the anger, and I used the word *grief,* which seemed to catch Gemma by surprise, as she had not associated her anger with grief

---

[3] Katz, "Knowing the Difference between Primary and Secondary Emotions Could Be the Key to Fighting Fairly with Your Partner."

at the time. I validated her expression of anger and asked what it felt like immediately after her husband told her about the affair.

"I felt angry," Gemma said.

"I know," I replied. "Now dig deeper. What else?"

"I mean, the anger came pretty fast." Head down and silent for a few thoughtful moments, Gemma then replied, "but I think my very first reaction was fear. Then I felt betrayed, and that led to the anger. I was so angry he betrayed me like that. That he would do that to our family."

Tears ran down her face. The heat the anger brought into the room was now cooled. We were moving through the grief process and having lightbulb moments.

It's common to have insight later in the grief process that the anger expressed may not have been logical, and from this discovery, one might feel guilty. However, I want to point out a classic cycle around anger when we are grieving. Thinking in the primary and secondary emotion sense, we feel anger, then we feel guilty about having that anger, which then leads to more anger. We can see this cycle with any emotion we feel in grief, though guilt is an interesting one that I will touch on in the following chapter. Take Adam*, for example, who has just lost his job. He feels angry that he was let go in the downsize of his company during the pandemic because he has been with the company for many years and is one of the top earners for his team. Because of that, Adam has been able to save money and realizes that he will be financially secure for a couple of months. He then feels guilty because other people who had earned less at the company are significantly struggling trying to find any type of job to hire them after the downsize. Even with that being true, Adam feels like the termination that forced him to go into his savings was unjust and ruins his vacation plans for later in the year now that he must use the money for rent....You see what I'm getting at here?

In the words of Dr. Seltzer:

If anger helps you feel in control, no wonder you can't control your anger![4]

---

[4] Selzer, "What your anger may be hiding."

Reponses from the research vividly painted a picture of how people encountered their grief-led anger. Responses ranged from wanting public revenge to dealing with one's anger privately. Many times, anger stretches across our world and relationships. Below are a few responses of different participants and how they express anger and who they express it to. Depending on, well ... a lot, we will have the impulse to outwardly or inwardly express anger that ends up manifesting as self-destruction.

"I felt numb. I felt angry and confused. I posted this as a comment on a picture of her current partner's Instagram post. I wanted her to have to say it out loud to someone. She had to tell someone how fucking disgusting a person she is. I wanted her to feel the same pain I felt."

Research participant, male, thirty-one, Texas

"Recently, I have been processing a lot of anger, which is being projected towards others. I expect people to fill a certain void within me without having to tell them how to fill it. I'm allowing myself to feel all these emotions because I know it's a part of the process, but deep down, I know this is going to affect me for the rest of my life. It's already changed me at my core."

Research participant, female, thirty-one, North Carolina

"I shut down completely. I felt nothing. And then, it all came back. Every time someone died, I questioned God; I got mad at God. I felt the grief of everyone else that had died."

Research participant, female, thirty-one, Maryland

"I could write pages about the guilt, the shame, the alcoholism, the self-injury, the suicidal gestures, the suicide attempt, the depression, the anxiety, the panic attacks, the disordered eating. But those things don't feel as relevant anymore."

Research participant, female, thirty-one, Maryland

"My experience with grief is very dark. It pertains to self-destruction nonetheless. Drugs, alcohol, lack of sleep and eating, sometimes suicidal thoughts. At the end of the day, the only thing that truly helps is a good support system. One that allows you to feel whatever it is you're feeling and being able to let that out."

Research participant, female, twenty-eight, Texas

I'm working with a first-time therapy client in his mid-thirties who had a goal to work through childhood trauma and explore how it shows up in his life as an adult. While working on this book, Earl* and I had a session that precisely modeled this emotional journey through anger regarding his grief process. Earl shared that since our last session, his late father's birthday had passed, and it had made him think about the relationship they would have had as Earl became an adult. He would want to ask his father a lot of questions and said he would then have someone to give him "manly advice," as Earl never had a person like this or someone to call on in his life. Identifying and exploring emotions has been a focal point of our work together, so I asked Earl if he was angry at his father.

"I can't be angry at him cause he isn't here to let him know or have a conversation. I want to be able to resolve it. That's probably why I get angry. I don't want to feel that way."

"What do you think the anger is doing for you?"

"Nothing. Not a damn thing."

"Are you sure? You aren't getting anything from the anger?"

"It's all I have to hold onto."

"Humm, so if you are 'holding on,' maybe it means you are afraid to let go? The anger seems to connect you to dad."

"It's connection, but I would rather connect on a positive note. Like connection because of love and not anger."

I reflect on past sessions where he told me about what it was like growing up in his home, not having significant amounts of parental supervision or care. I asked Earl if he can remember doing things when he was a child that he knew he shouldn't, and what would happen afterward when his parents found out. Broadening this, why any child he knew might act out in challenging environments and what would follow.

"They get their ass whipped, but it's still getting attention. It's like a dog. I'm seen; I'm being seen." Earl lets out a laugh that seems to have a hint of sadness. "I'm just a little kid that's trying to get attention, and it sucks because it's gone."

I share that when children don't get the attention they need from a caregiver, they can infer that when they do get the attention in a negative form or even abuse, the child might think, "At least it's something....My parent *cares enough* to give attention to 'whip my ass.'" I make it clear that this can be a thought process of a growing brain, and abusing a child is never love.

Earl agrees and takes time to process.

In reflection, I ask, "So, if this was your experience in childhood, from parent to child and anger meaning that there's care, maybe your anger represents you still care enough about dad to be angry at him."

"Anger is connection, even though I find it hard to be angry at anyone. But if I let go, I'm going to losing something I really never got. It's hard to accept."

"Is there anything else to represent connection besides anger?"

"Love. I didn't see it or feel it all the time, but I knew it was there. It's hard to go to that when you don't genuinely know. We get caught up in hearing someone verbally say something to believe it."

"Did you hear your dad ever say that he loved you?"

"I didn't ever hear it from him. Even on his death bed, I told him I loved him, and he said, 'I know.' I'm just assuming it's the show no love emotions. But it can't be like that."

"What do you think of the 'show no love emotions'?"

"That shit's stupid. When you aren't taught that it's okay to show emotion, you get stuck in that." There's directness in Earl's voice as if talking to his father. Shaking his head in disappointment, he says, "You leave that in the streets; don't take that home. There needs to be somewhere you take the cape off."

I share with Earl that I have gone to see mediums in the past in hopes of getting answers and relief from the grief I have experienced: "When I went, I had a really wonderful experience that made me feel that what I was told was true and sincere. The thing is, though, I had no hard proof of this, but believing it made me feel better. When I tell people I am into talking with mediums, I get some eye rolls, and I get it; they think it's bullshit. But if it brings solace to my pain, does it matter if it's bullshit or not?"

"No. It doesn't matter what other people think of it or if it's true. If you believe it's true or it makes you feel better, that's all that counts."

"Right. So, even if you don't genuinely know for sure if your father loved you, and he isn't here to ask now, what is the harm in believing that he did if it brings you comfort and peace?"

"Yeah. It's my universe and what I choose to believe. If I chose to believe that it was a loving environment, then that's what matters. We can choose what and who we allow in our universe. It's about making our world have meaning."

I recapitulate the session as Earl and I come to the end, sharing that he went from denial and invalidating feelings of anger towards his father to becoming curious and moving through the emotions by connecting with his inner child. Earl ends with acceptance of his own feelings and using the middle path to recognize that though there was a lot of things that should not have happened to Earl as a child, believing that love still existed in the environment encourages movement through complicated grief.

***

Many participants in the research shared about the shockingness of grief. Going through a loss and the intense emotions that join along like a one-two sucker punch, some might say. When I think about how this feels, I can viscerally remember what I felt like after a really intense cry, fully using my body to let out emotion. It felt like I was hit by a damn bus, so fierce that there must be some physical proof of assault. Then remembering it's "just" grief.

```
"I used to believe that grief would be a
linear progression. That one day you would
   emerge from the dark heavy feeling that
   surrounds you. After several years, I am
still stunned, sometimes, by the swift punch
to the gut that can come from nowhere. The
grief lurks in the dark corners, and though
it no longer brings me to my knees, it has
```

the power to erase all the progress I feel I have made, at least temporarily. Now, there are more good days than bad, and the hole in my heart continues to become smaller. That to me is progress in my grief."

Research participant, female, sixty, Maryland

"I was so busy taking care of everyone else in my family that I never dealt with my own grief. It hit me like a cement wall. My chest was heavy. Tears fell for the first time in a year. I mourned that day for his life and my life without him. This past year without him, I have thought about him every day, but I thought about getting my grandmother 'through this' more."

Research participant, female, twenty-five, New Jersey

"When the unexpected happens—it is like being punched in the face out of nowhere. You get accustomed to how things have been and how life feels comfortable—so when something uncomfortable comes—it disrupts your thought process and causes waves of emotion and anxiety."

Research participant, female, thirty-seven, Texas

"What to say about grief ... depends on the day, how I'm feeling, whether or not grief has decided to strike today. Even the people around me can set it off. Today, I'm good; grief isn't bothering me at the moment. But I have come to learn that grief is like an earworm. You never know when it's going to appear, and you don't know how long it's going to last. My grief likes to show up in the form of nightmares. Not necessarily scary but situations that make me so angry I wake up sweating, teeth clenched and often ready to throw punches. My nightmares are always the same. I'm with my mom (who died five years ago), and I'm trying to talk to her, but she won't look at me, acknowledge me, or speak to me. Then I get so angry, I begin to yell at her, scream at her, and often curse at her. This probably sounds like no big deal, but in my mom's final weeks, the cancer must have been in her brain, because forming thoughts and sentences became harder and harder for her. We couldn't talk anymore. She couldn't tell me what she wanted or what she needed. I had to guess. Then, she couldn't talk at all. She was awake but just looked at you.

"I'm almost certain this is where these nightmares stem from. She was in home hospice for a few months before she passed, and the nurses tried to give us a heads-up on what to expect, but this wasn't one of them. No one told me I wasn't able to talk to my mom in her final weeks/days. I don't know if she heard me, let alone understood me. Everyone kept telling me to say whatever I needed or wanted to say to her so things didn't go "unsaid," but I still feel like I missed my window of opportunity because her mental state went slowly, and I wasn't prepared. I still spoke to her, asked her what she wanted, if she was cold, if she was thirsty, but I often got [a] random phrase from her instead of a response."

Research participant, female, twenty-nine, Maryland

Imagine painting with watercolors. The untarnished blank canvas is laid out in front of you. This piece of canvas represents your life. Next to it, you have an assortment of colors to choose from. Each has its own story to tell. You take the paintbrush, and that is next to your cup of water, meant to wash away a story and prepare for a new one. Dipping the paintbrush into the water, gently, purposefully, the bristles soaking in the moisture to prepare for the process. You first wet the canvas, letting the water seep through the layers of your life. Then you gaze at the freedom of colors to choose. You pick one. Tenderly sweeping the brush back and forth until sufficiently full. Then, in the middle of the canvas, you make a pin-size drop of color and watch what happens. Placing the paintbrush in the cup of water to wash away the now-somewhat-stained brush. When it drips clear, you soak the bristles again, filling them up. You move the brush over to the canvas, and you let a droplet fall on top of your color, maybe another, then another.

What you see happening is the diffusion of color, noticing the most concentrated area becomes lighter shades of the color as it extends further. The color is ...

Your loss
Your trigger
Your trauma
Your anger
Your grief.

This, though, is a small hit. Spreads across your life, but not far.

Now you go back to your selection of colors and vigorously dance the paintbrush around until vivid pigment is dripping off. Going back to your canvas, you find the middle again and this time let the pigment leave a bigger, deeper, seeping-through-the-canvas mark. You add water. What happens?

When grief arrives after a loss in our lives, we feel the great impact of the contrast when it attacks the center of who we are. The bigger the grief, the wider it spreads, and more of our life is affected. The loss, trigger, trauma, anger is the middle. The people, relationships, and responsibilities closest to us continue to get a significantly concentrated piece of the grief. Following the patterned chaos, it becomes more diluted and has a smaller effect on the things that are far away from our center yet still overwhelmingly runs off the sides.

To help you control the run-off, here are some suggestions on what to do with that anger.

Consider it. Is anger a stand-in for more painful emotions, or does the situation warrant it? Do you feel abandoned or afraid? If so, could you enlist support from others or spend some time thinking about your fears and putting them to rest? It might help to share your feelings in a grief support group and learn how others have dealt with similar feelings.

Express it. Set aside a safe time and place each day to defuse angry feelings. Some people yell in the car with the windows rolled up. Some find stress-relief techniques like meditation or yoga helpful. Others find release in punching pillows or in spurts of strenuous activity. Think about options for releasing anger, and plan how to express it safely when it crops up. Sometimes writing about situations that make you feel angry can help you identify and focus on what you are really feeling beneath your anger.

12

The Taste of Tears

"**M**y largest amount of grief I've ever experienced was losing my first dog after ten years. I said out loud multiple times that I was prepared and that I understood that he was getting older and that I would be okay, but when it happened, I was not. First, I had to make the decision to put him down, as he stopped walking or really living at all, and that feeling of playing 'God' with something you love is very difficult. Secondly, I was unable to accept that I was losing something so close that loved me unconditionally. There is no love like a pet because you are their only. They love you no matter what, and you forget that as time passes with them. You take advantage of the time with them because it's so consistent until it isn't, and then it's a harsh reality that they are gone and never coming back. I struggled to accept that he was a 'once in a lifetime' pet. I don't think I'll be able to bond as closely with another pet because Bettis and I grew up together and moved across the country twice. I now know that it is a blessing to have experienced it at all, but when I lost him, I couldn't accept it. Finally, I felt very alone in my grief because no one spent as much time, energy, or money with him as I did, and so, when people were sad for me, I felt like they weren't as sad as me, and that bothered me a lot. Particularly from my partner—I felt like he could never give me enough of what I needed at that time because he just didn't love Bettis as much as I did. I now know that it was grief-stricken thoughts to put that pressure on him because he wasn't his dog, so how would he get it? But at the time, it was very difficult. I cried multiple times a week from June 2020 until January 2021 and was told by medical professionals that I was depressed from the situation combined with a new role, but losing Bettis was the core. I still don't think I've accepted that I'll never see him again and am not religious in nature. I can see where people turn to religion when you're grieving because if I could see him again, I would give anything, and most would say I'll see him in heaven. I just am not sold on that, so I'll just miss him and appreciate what we had."

Research participant, female, thirty-one, Texas

Sadness is a hallmark symptom of grief and can come into our lives in so many circumstances and show up in so many ways. Non-exhaustively, illustrations include silent weeping, withdrawal and isolation, crying on the shoulder of a supportive friend, or the full-body presentation of mourning that floods your system, and no matter how exodus-like the sorrow is, there is always more. A common fear that I hear from a lot from people who I speak to about grief is that they are afraid to "let it out" due to the fear of not being able to contain it back up. The old "if I start, then I won't be able to stop." A valid *and* totally illogical fear. The truth is that we *will* eventually stop; we just aren't told the timeline ahead of time. The real or assumed loss of agency over our body, mind, and emotions is something that is incredibly difficult to tolerate and comprehend. This all comes back to our loss of control ... which, you guessed it, you also grieve. One way we take this control back is deciding how we will show up in grief: loudly or quietly?

"In my mind, I think I'm okay when I think about my father, even when someone asks about him, but as soon as I open my mouth, I start to cry, no matter who I'm talking to. It's been seven months since he passed away. I dream about him maybe once or twice a month, and every time, it's so perfect and makes me so happy, keeps me going. I know I carry this grief with me. It's heavy. The hardest part of it, all of that, [was] I didn't get to say goodbye [and] had no warning what was happening. I feel like I'm in one of those crazy TV shows sometimes. Like, how is this happening to me, to him?"

Research participant, female, twenty-nine, Massachusetts

"When he passed, I was a puddle. And in some ways, I still am. I don't feel as secure, safe, or confident as used to. Since his passing, I've gotten a good taste of what depression and anxiety feel like. I've had many recent nights of curling into a ball and crying on the floor. Or feeling too insecure to be in social situations. I usually try to pretend he's still alive, and I just haven't seen him in a while. That's when I feel a little more whole and complete. When I don't pretend, I feel scared and lost. That's my life now. I've been in therapy, started taking meds, but that looming sadness is still there if I think about it for too long. I'm afraid of life now almost as much as I am afraid of death."

Research participant, female, twenty-seven, Texas

I am often asked what the difference is between depression, grief, and sadness. Here's the 411:

Depression is a diagnosable disorder, often due to genes and life events that lead to a chemical imbalance of neurotransmitters in the brain. However, depression doesn't always have a "direct cause." Hopelessness, decreased acts of daily living, little interest in pleasurable activities, and/or thoughts of death or suicide can occur. Both grief and sadness could turn into depression, so seeking professional help in the form of therapy and/or medication can be useful forms to combat symptoms.[1]

---

[1] Healthwise Staff, "Depression."

Grief is a natural response to a loss. When we are grieving, we are going through a process of adjustment that can include feelings of sadness, heartbreak, and loss of focus. Grief is a unique experience for each person and doesn't have a timeline. Generally, good social and relational support through personal or professional systems can help someone through their grief.

Sadness is a typical and necessary emotion that is regularly felt by people. It is a useful emotion that can help us empathize with ourselves or others and express pain or tension we emotionally feel. Sadness is what you felt when you were watching the scene in Air Bud where Josh is yelling at Buddy, telling him, "Get out of here! Don't you understand?! Get! I don't want you anymore!"[2] A true splash zone.

"My grief has manifested in emotional eating, drinking, and clinical depression, lack of motivation, and crying at random times."

Research participant, female, thirty-one, Georgia

"I think the initial grief has turned into more anxiety-like symptoms that have manifested itself into the things I can't control."

Research participant, female, twenty-eight, California

---

[2] Your Family Entertainment, "Air Bud."

"The weeks before leaving Melbourne, I felt
like I was crying on the hour every hour. I
kept thinking to myself, *I don't know when
and if I do return to this place, but if I
ever do return, it is not going to ever be
the place that I left behind. Things will
happen; people will move on.*"

*Research participant, female, thirty-two,
London*

Reinforcing the curious rather than judgmental perspective, why is feeling sadness important in grief? Most of us would think it favorable if we could "just skip over that sad shit and get the show on the road," as I had a client once tell me. In addition to the proceeding details about how sadness functions as a reset to the brain, a valuable role of sadness represents the reason why I think most people want to avoid it: it forces us to pause and look inward. Sadness promotes inner reflection, which is helpful in our journey to acceptance. Physiological arousal decreases, allowing our body and brain to rest to "update cognitive structures and to accommodate lost objects." When we allow ourselves to experience sadness, we are rewarded with an opportunity to reassess goals and plans.[3]

Guilt is an interesting emotion. Similarly to shame, it can be hard to recognize the function of these emotions, especially because these are often seen as negative and detrimental emotions. Feeling guilt when we are grieving can be very informative to our emotional situation. We feel guilt for three main reasons. First, we have guilt because we actually did something wrong. Making mistakes is human, and the intensity of those mistakes ranges, though sometimes those mistakes can have very impactful consequences,

---

[3] Bananno, Goorin, and Coifman, "Sadness and Grief."

such as leading to a death. Second, we feel guilty because we feel like we did something wrong. Just because you feel guilty doesn't mean you are. As we know, our feelings that we experience in grief can be irrational and consuming. The third reason we feel guilt with grief is because we want order. This one hits deep for most of us. If we don't have someone or something to blame, then we must accept that the world is unpredictable and disorderly. However, if we think we could have done something differently to therefore change an outcome, we provide ourselves solace that there is rational order, and we have some sort of control. Even the perception of control falls into this. Accepting that there was no way to have known or change the outcome is admitting that there are things outside of our control, which can be a hard thing to comprehend. Holding onto control means holding onto hope. So, after losing so much already, no wonder why it's devastating to think we can lose our hope too.[4]

I am a visual learner, so I will often create some kind of visual depiction for myself when learning new concepts. If this would be helpful for a client that I'm working with as well, I will do my best to give a detailed visualization or pull out my dry erase board. I've done this when describing a common theme around guilt: too much or not enough. For example, too sad vs. not sad enough, talking about the loss too much vs. feeling guilty for not bringing it up, not wanting to stay in the pain forever vs. "getting over" the loss too soon. A tricky paradox that grief loves to pull on us. Many people I've worked with describe going through this and find it frustrating, confusing, and frankly, exhausting. So, I have come up with a visual:

There are two islands in the middle of a body of water. One represents "too much," and the other represents "not enough." When we are grieving, we can swim back and forth one hundred times a day, feeling more and more exhausted. The water in between the islands is the guilt we feel, encouraging us to swim faster to the opposite piece of land. Eventually, we notice there is actually a third island way in the distance and directly between the first two islands. The water separating the two islands from the third is a bit choppier

---

[4] Williams, "Guilt and Grief: Coping with the Shoulda, Woulda, Couldas."

and represents survival. Because when we surpass our feelings of guilt, we can notice our head is above water, and we are surviving. Finally, we are able to dock at the third island of acceptance, compassion, and middle ground.

This, too, can represent an anomaly; what about survivor's guilt? I was surprised to not see more responses from the research give examples of how and why some participants experience this, as it often comes up in talk therapy. My client Gia would often talk about feeling guilty that her husband was taken and not her, telling me he was the "better person."

"I'm a combat veteran, and every day, I have survivor's guilt. Also, PTSD and most of my grief comes from the deaths of my friends who became family to me. Also, friends that committed suicide due to their demons getting the best of them. I came to the realization that this will never go away, ever. I talk to other veterans and try to help them."

Research participant, male, thirty-seven, Maryland

"They are interconnected; guilt is being here and being the one who survived."

Therapy client

The desire for order seems to come out in both quotes—desiring that we had more control in events that led to the death of someone we cared about. Survivor's guilt can also be portrayed in the way we speak about ourselves through negative self-talk. When we have a sense of responsibility or wrestle with how or why something happened, we may not even feel worthy of seeking help. Comparing oneself to others, feeling guilt for feeling the way we do, or grieving in the way we are because of the relationship we had with the person is only cyclical. Recognizing that we have choice in what we do with the guilt we feel can create healing for others and ourselves.

Guilt can be shocking to feel while grieving for people who haven't experienced significant grief before. Guilt may come up for those who are watching others grieve as well, which is no easy task. I've discovered that being a witness to someone's pain and their grief is quite profound, which is why I always have felt honored for people to share their narrative with me in the therapeutic space. At the same time, when we are grieving ourselves, witnessing others grieve can be all too much and create a pattern of suffering.

"Everything turned upside down from that night forward. My parents divorced, my father left, and I had to put on a happy facade to take care of my mother, who became a shell of a person. I think this is when I became hardened. People called me "strong." Trauma and complicated grief do different things to different people. Crying was weakness; I couldn't shed tears in front of my mom. I had to be the "strong" one and try to hold the falling pieces of my life together to salvage any remains of a family that we had left. It just became my mom and me. In a lot of ways, I think it just became me. Shakespeare said it best: 'As two spent

swimmers that do cling together/And choke
their art.' We were drowning in our grief,
and we were drowning each other."

*Research participant, female, thirty-one,
Maryland*

When enduring deep grief, we might call it suffering. I have seen and heard many views of suffering through recounts of others, articles, and research. I often come across the point of view that pain is inevitable, while suffering is a choice we make. While I do think that is objectively true, it doesn't validate the experience we have, and it doesn't leave room for the gray. I was once told by a therapist of my own that medication helps with the suffering so therapy can work on the pain. I think about this often, and while recognizing that medication is a personal choice and should be discussed with their doctor, I share it with clients who are considering medication as part of their treatment plan. This perspective beautifully illustrates that suffering often is a barrier to processing the grief, trauma, or pain.

Pain is the activation of the nervous system that signals distress by sensory and emotional experience. It's the unavoidable response to harm that can be influenced by cognitive and neurological factors. To some, pain can also be motivating. Suffering is distinctly psychological and resulting from the existential meaning one gives to their encounter of pain. Noam Shpancer, Ph.D. shares how tolerating short-term pain prevents long-term suffering. A fundamental piece to healthy behavior management is this: challenges exist, and to overcome them, they require being met. Prevailing short-term discomfort is the bridge to long-term health and adaptation. "Those who cannot tolerate acute temporary discomfort now condemn themselves to chronic suffering later."[5]

Generally, we don't consciously choose to suffer. Yet, we end up doing so because we are afraid that if we don't, we could

---

[5] Shpancer, "Laws of Emotional Mastery."

experience the loss of memories with a loved one, not feel validation in our grief from others, or have the belief that suffering will honor the person we lost. Tolerating the reality of loved ones no longer being with us can feel insufferable.

"I don't think I quite understand, even at twenty-eight, that death is forever, and they are never coming back, and how you need to accept it when it comes (in a designated timeframe) and then move on. But properly handling it is very critical for healing."

Research participant, female, thirty-one, Texas

"Grief is a weird thing. One day, someone is here, and the next, they're not, and you just get to keep on living and have to figure out how to fill a space you never thought would be empty before. That's a very clinical way of describing the pain that comes with loss. Time passes, and you just function and survive and suppress and try not to be triggered in public or at work or at the wrong times."

Research participant, female, thirty-one, Maryland

"They've each made me sensitive to different
    subjects over the years, and I'll find
myself being triggered by a conversation or
TV show or song and feel fucked up about it
            for days afterward."

Research participant, female, thirty, Texas

We might feel a subconscious need to increase suffering when we experience triggers in our grief. The anniversary of a death or a birthday of a deceased loved one frequently is seen as a day that can be triggering. When starting therapy with someone who has experienced a trauma or loss, I asked them about dates or times of the year events occurred. That way, I can be aware of more dysregulation or increased negative or dangerous thoughts at this time. I do a lot of coping ahead with clients to prepare for these times. During this time, there is no "right" way to act or "right" thing to do. It's normal for people to have to take off work, either because they want the personal time to reflect and grieve or because of an inability to function. Some may do something special or just live like any other day, remembering that there is no wrong choice. Because of our pain or suffering, choosing what to do on these days can feel like the heaviest decision in the world. I frequently find that we put the meaning of our entire relationship on this day. I encourage people to give themselves compassion, knowing that whatever decision they make will be the right one.

"So, I recently just lost my mom to ALS, and what I found was I started grieving the moment she got sick. I grieved for the missed vacations and the missed normalcy. I grieved because I didn't know what else to do! I fought with her, and I was so angry and frustrated and bitter. I was embroiled in the very stereotypical "five stages of grief." My mom raised me as a single parent, and all I knew how to do was try my hardest to fight the battle for her and push her to fight. But what I found was that I couldn't make the decision for her, which made my grief even greater. It's so hard to grieve for someone who is still alive because it makes the pain even greater. It's even harder to watch someone you love waste away to nothing, knowing that they won't see you grow to be the person that they want you to become, or you want to become. It also sucked that while there are groups for young adults of cancer patients in their twenties, there is no support group for caregivers of ALS patients in their twenties, and trust me, my friends, while supportive, were helpful and loving and amazing in this arena, but not always the most....well, they didn't always get it! Their parents weren't sick. I don't blame them! This shit sucks. My mom went from working sixty hours in the city to bedbound and a feeding tube in four months, and dead six months later.

"I felt alone. I grieved because I felt alone. My mom had an illness that was terminal. I grieved because I had nowhere to turn, because my mom couldn't talk, because she couldn't leave her bed, because I couldn't leave her, because when I did (I went away on two short trips last summer, with family watching her) she ended up in the hospital. I grieved because I felt immense guilt constantly (I still get the guilts!). Talk about being in your twenties and trying to have a life when you can't even go out to dinner. I couldn't visit friends. I put my life on hold. Keep in mind I wouldn't change a damn thing—my mom was and is my best friend—but her illness and her death taught me more than I could ever imagine.

"Takeaway: In the two and a half years that my mom was sick, I found that I grieved far more and far quicker during her actual illness than I grieved after she actually passed (to be fair, at this moment, it's only been eight weeks), which to me sounds so horrifying yet normal.

"When she passed at the end of March, I was relieved and didn't grieve until nearly a month later when the dust settled again, and I saw how much of the world she shut out in her own grief. She didn't want people to see her illness, so she hid away for the majority of her illness until her death. I could never imagine living like that, and yet, I watched and enabled her to do that for two and a half years."

Research participant, female, thirty, Pennsylvania

13

Hello?!

Can't You See I'm Grieving?!

"My most recent experience of grief started when a good friend ended her life in July 2019. It's all-consuming at times and barely there at others. I feel guilt when I don't feel the loss as presently, and I feel guilt when I feel it in an all-consuming way. Who am I to claim all of this grief? She wasn't my daughter or my sister or my lover; she was my friend. My grief doesn't matter. Intellectually, I know that's bullshit, but grief is weird. For me, grief has been like wearing a heavy jacket you can never take off. I thought if I wore it long enough, I'd stop feeling its weight. Sometimes, I even think I might have grown used to it. But then, suddenly and all at once, it feels so heavy I think I'll suffocate. And I nearly do. To some degree, I'm hoping for that suffocating feeling because it connects me to her and gives me somewhere to put my love for her."

Research participant, female, thirty-four, Florida

To love is to grieve.

To grieve is to love.

I will frequently use my whiteboard to draw the following for my clients:

At the top, there is an arrangement of negative coping mechanisms: substance use, avoidance, isolation, self-injury, disordered eating, codependence, emotional dysregulation, etc.

Then a thick dark line of separation.

Below the line, an arrangement of symptoms, experiences, or emotions we are trying to push down: grief, trauma, anxiety, depression, "I'm not good enough," "I'm worthless," etc.

I will then explain that we often use what we have up top to protect us, when what is below the line feels threating. When you're in therapy, those negative coping mechanisms will be challenged and encouraged to not be in your life anymore.

I start to lightly swipe the eraser across the top and middle of the board, slowly diminishing the words and the thick barrier.

Simultaneously, drawing squiggly lines from the arrangement of symptoms, experiences, and emotions in an upwards fashion.

I explain that when we are new to therapy and new to the work, it's not uncommon to feel like things are getting worse before they get better. I'll say to the client, "Here I come, taking what you have used to manage and protect yourself, and be like ... 'nah,' and try to then take them away! How rude of me."

Of course, this doesn't happen all at once, and along the way, healthy coping skills are being built. Though what I and colleagues have seen in clients is that not too long after beginning therapy, maybe one to three months, symptoms could get worse. Have no fear! We prepared for this.

This is not only a paradoxical paradigm for many mental health disorders that one might come to therapy for but also very much describes the paradoxical paradigm of grief. There are so many illustrations of this. For example, for something that everyone experiences, grief sure is lonely. Commonly hearing this as *being alone in a crowded room,* we probably all know the feeling. At some point, though, we could look around and question this like, *dang, there's a lot of people in here....Why do I feel so damn lonely!?* Without taking a curious perspective to this, it can lead to more feelings of loneliness and isolation. Another example of a grief paradox is how we continue a relationship with the person who is now deceased. Writing letters to Drew after his death or continuing to talk about him in the present tense represents this well. Acknowledging that the "stages of grief"[1] are not stages at all, as they do not necessarily go in order, nor do we experience all of them when grieving. In fact, this book is a paradox. Sure, the intention was set and communicated that I am sharing my own experience, especially in the first half of the book. Part Two is a broader experience, though still edited by my personal lens. When anyone talks about grief, even providing theory backed up by research, the consumer of the information will always have a uniquely individual experience. Just because millions of people experience a "symptom" of grief doesn't guarantee that you will. In that case, what is even the point in finishing reading this book....

---

[1] Kubler-Ross, *On Death and Dying.*

....Still with me? If you couldn't handle the suspense, welcome back.

More often than not, one of the paradoxes seen in grief is how we relate to others who are simultaneously grieving either the same loss or a different one. There is a familiar expectation for others to fill a void that now exists within our new grief-filled bodies. We will want others, especially those close to us, to know how to help us in our grief and what to do to either make us feel better or process and move forward. We might expect people in our lives to grieve the way we do in a collective loss or "sympathy grieve" in solidarity. When these seemingly illogical requests or expectations are not received, it can feel devastating to us, like another loss. For others, the loneliness can feel unbearable, *and* even when people try and support us, we say they just can't understand what we're going through push them away. We become protective and have a desire to have unique grief, finding comfort in the "specialness" and that our grief is different from others. We even compare our loss or our grief to others, attempting to find validation in superiority—*who is in more pain?* The paradox of being in so much pain, wishing you weren't, yet being terrified of that pain leaving. Giving arbitrary meaning to the pain or suffering continuing: *if I'm in pain, then I miss him; I remember him; I love him; he's with me.* I wonder if this becomes a barrier to healing. Because yes—it's so unpleasant, and *now* we know what it feels like. It's now familiar and strangely comfortable. Bringing it back to identity, not being *okay* is our new norm, and everything else feels like a threat. À la, *the devil you know vs. the devil you don't.*

"He died twenty years ago May 3, and I still miss him, and I still have things of his I should throw away. But I have not done it. Most people get completely stuck there—removing personal stuff is like divorcing the person after they are dead."

Research participant, female, sixty-five, California

"I have an interesting relationship with grief. Some losses have been heartbreaking, and others I had a very difficult relationship with and felt nothing....Those who I miss the most though continue to live in my thoughts. I constantly feel them with me as I go throughout my days. I write about them; I talk to them in my head. I treasure items that have been given to me that were theirs."

Research participant, female, twenty-nine, Texas

"Writing about grief was like watching my drama-horror movie life."

Research participant, feminine, Québec

Early on in the grief process, we often don't think thankfulness and gratitude party with grief. *Well, think again!* There is a difference between thankfulness and gratitude: being thankful is a feeling, while being grateful is an action. Both exist within our grief, and it's our job to find it. We might do this when we create meaning from a loss or when our story becomes a survival guide to another. We can extend gratitude for someone or something that has been in our life *and* still feel the immense cavity that resulted from the loss. It's not a silver lining; silver linings are about the *yeah, but*; *so far*; *at least.*

I regularly experience this paradox as a therapist. Though it may be surprising, termination of a therapeutic relationship is often tough for the therapist and not just for the client. Many therapists will talk about termination from the first session, not in a pessimistic way but in an honest, ethical, and relational way. This is a relationship that will come to an end, as all do, though the

228 Adding the E

therapeutic one is unlike any other. For a subjectively limited timeframe, you share a significant amount of time and intimacy with another person who you don't necessarily have anything in common with besides your schedules lining up for an hour a week and some sort of supply and demand. As I have probably overstated already, I have cosmic gratitude and thankfulness for what I do as a profession. I care deeply for my clients, and seeing them succeed to the point of not "needing" me anymore is a triumph and difficult at times, even sorrowful. Though like love and grief, one can't exist without the other.

Acknowledging that there are numerous paradoxes in grief, it's essential to acknowledge the power of a reframe. I smirk when writing this, as I think about my response to clients I have healthy rapport with when I want them to reframe something they just said: "Try again." I say it like this because I think it's funny, and I usually get a half-annoyed/half-humorous response back. But also ... seriously ... *try again.* The amount of sass I lay out with this also depends on the shape of the rapport.

Reframing language and thoughts can be metamorphic, especially when it comes to grief and death. As aforementioned, when we think that suffering will bring integrity to pain and loss, we end up honoring the pain and suffering rather than honoring who or what was lost. One of the times this had the most impetus in my grief was when I thought that my creativity would leave if I didn't feel or connect to my pain. It was Jordan, my speaking coach, that reminded me that pain and suffering did not equal love. Sometimes, you can hear something over and over or cognitively know something to be true but just can't connect with it. I guess I was in the right space that day when she said those words because it changed my grieving process. I no longer felt like I had to be in deep pain in order to continue to love Drew. A revelation to a resolution.

Complicated grief, comprised of disenfranchised grief and ambiguous loss, is especially paradoxical. When we have a broadly complicated relationship with those who were lost in our lives, it's hard to know what our grief should look like or if there will even be a grief process.

"I've had some interesting deaths occur in my life. Namely, several of my enemies have died. My own rapist died in a motorcycle accident, and my best friend's rapist died in a car accident. A woman I'd been close to in the past who went on to cause emotional pain for myself and other friends later completed suicide. A guy who attempted to assault me while I was on drugs ended up dying in a car accident. I've always joked that if you hurt me, you could die. I find it funny, because if I don't, it's sad, and I'd rather not deal with that."

Research participant, female, thirty, Texas

Knowing a significant loss is coming, already anticipatory grieving, doesn't always make the loss less painful or shocking.

"I think my grief is different than what people tend to think of it as....usually, they feel grief is "after the fact"—but I disagree. I am grieving because I know that my babies will not outlive me. I am grieving because I am watching the decline in health and behavioral changes— especially this past year. It is hard watching your fur kids become different souls. They are no longer able to walk as long, they have health issues popping up here and there, one has Alzheimer's and has his good and bad days—for example, today is one of his bad days, as he looks lost and scared. His

vision and hearing have declined
greatly....So, I am grieving for him and for
her—because they can't tell me what is
hurting or what they're thinking or how
they're feeling. They may still be here on
earth—but who they are—are here every now
and then—on their good days."

Research participant, female, thirty-seven,
Texas

A miscarriage is a profound disenfranchised loss. People in my life that I care about very dearly have experienced this misunderstood and isolating loss. Participants of the research share their own narrative around enduring a miscarriage. It felt imperative to highlight the following three experiences of losing children in ways that individuals are deprived of the right to grieve: two portrayals from the research on these women's sudden loss of an unborn child and one woman's experience of the painful grief that comes with being a foster parent.

"I found out my unborn child has a rare
chromosome abnormality called triploidy,
which is not compatible with life and can be
life-threatening for the mother if carried
full term. I had to make the difficult
decision to terminate a wanted pregnancy at
fifteen weeks. The grief is unlike anything
I have ever felt before, heavy and sometimes
paralyzing with a steady stream of tears

anytime I think about the decision I had to make for myself and my daughter. She never had a chance at the life I imagined for my child since I was a child, and that is sometimes too heavy to handle. Recently, I have been processing a lot of anger, which is being projected towards others. I expect people to fill a certain void within me without having to tell them how to fill it. I'm allowing myself to feel all these emotions because I know it's a part of the process, but deep down, I know this is going to affect me for the rest of my life. It's already changed me at my core."

Research participant, female, thirty-two, North Carolina

"On October 8 of 2019, I was [awoken] out of my sleep at 4 a.m. I was having severe pain. Cramps were on one thousand. I've never felt anything like this before. I was crying and rocking myself in fetal position. I got up and took a hot shower, hoping the heat would bring me some relief, but none. We had our first prenatal appointment that morning, but before we could make it there, I had a miscarriage at home. I felt like I had to use the bathroom, and all the sudden, I felt this ball-like thing come out. I miscarried my baby on the toilet, THE FUCKING TOILET! In movies, when someone has a miscarriage, they show all this blood, and in real life, that's exactly how it was. Just bleeding, heavy, nonstop. You would've thought I was stabbed or shot. It was a crime scene in the bathroom. This was an unreal heartbreak I experienced. I've heard other stories of ladies having miscarriages, but I never thought it would've happened to me. My sisters had successful pregnancies, so I just assumed the same for me. I've never cried so hard and so much in my life. So many emotions flushed me; it was just overwhelming. I felt unworthy, disappointment, anger, unfit, confused. Like, how could this happen to me? What did I do or didn't do to deserve this? It just felt unfair. In present time, I have been able to accept this experience. I know this experience has a purpose to bless my life and others.

Research participant, female, thirty, Maryland

There was an area of grief that I was surprised to not hear about from any of the participants of the research. No evidence showed that any of the participants had personal experience with the foster care system—no shared evidence, at least. This is one of the reasons why I thought it would be important to talk about and share a perspective of a client of mine who has experience as a foster parent with her husband. When I asked Rilee* how she felt about me adding some of her story, she seemed eager to have more information out in the world to validate the heartache that is involved and often not recognized or deeply misunderstood.

When I first started seeing Rilee, she and Avi* were fostering twin toddler girls who they completely fell in love with. The hope was that they were going to be able to adopt the girls in the future. Though the stress of a parent was challenging to manage at times, as any parent knows, the love and joy Rilee had for her role and the twins was above and beyond any challenge. Rilee would talk in session about the difficulty to be validated by others as a "real" mother. I saw the pain and rejection she experienced when the biological mothers of children at the daycare left her out of things, or when Rilee's family didn't refer to her and Avi as parents and the twins as their children.

About two months into working together, Rilee told me that a "possibility" was confirmed and that the girls were being placed with a biological family member sooner than later, and her grief process had already started. The foster care system is chaotic, and there are often a lot of unknowns when it comes to foster care placements and children being moved. Rilee was in a very tough place, as she had competing feelings: feeling the deep grief of the loss of these children that had been in their lives for longer than they had even expected due to the rise of COVID-19 and knowing that safe family reunification is a goal in the foster care system. Rilee just wanted what was best for these little girls. The next few months and especially over the Thanksgiving holiday, Rilee was sharply feeling her grief as the twins moved closer to an unknown departure date and were spending more time with their biological family on weekend visitations.

Rilee would often share how difficult it was to be a foster parent, and the range of the emotions were brutal. In a particularly emotional session, Rilee talked about the lack of support she has felt from the people in her life and stated, "There are so many little things that no one tells you about that make this so much harder." The fatiguing task of grieving the loss of her children while she was parenting them in the last couple of weeks was uniquely intense. When the children left, an assortment of emotions came to the surface: sadness, relief, heartbreak….

Since Rilee and Avi lost the twins, Rilee's grief has shown up in unexpected ways: "random" sadness, feelings of guilt, throwing herself into work, and feeling reactive or numb. Similar to the research participants' responses, Rilee felt isolated in her grief. She found it hard to share her grief with others and was often unable to talk about it with the support she had in her life. As others have stated as well, the amount of support decreased over even a short amount of time for Rilee and Avi, increasing feelings of shame and loneliness in her grief. Rilee has continued to grieve the loss of her foster children, though recently, the grief considerably reentered her mind when there was a desperate need of a placement for an infant, and Rilee and Avi were asked if they could take the child. In Rilee's experiences, when foster parents are asked if they would like a child placed with them, they are put in a position to decide in very little time with extremely limited information.

Due to the uncertainty of the foster care process, foster parents don't know if they are stepping into lifelong parenting or if they will have a child for the weekend. When I met next with Rilee, it was a very difficult and grief-filled session. Rilee and Avi were asked if they could take the infant. After deciding they would, Rilee and Avi had to prepare: get their home baby-ready, borrowing items from friends, canceling plans and telling others why, taking time off work, emotionally preparing for caring for a baby ... and all of this happened in less than a week. Having said that, hours before we started our session that day, and less than forty-eight hours until the child would be in their arms, she got a call saying that there was either a chance the placement would fall through, the child was going to be with them for a very short amount of time, or everything was going to go as scheduled.

Now, in foster parent limbo, the only thing Rilee could do was wait in a pool of pain and uncertainty. Rilee would tell me that her friends ask why she puts herself through this. "They have a point," she tells me. Melancholic in session, Rilee says she jinxed herself. She shouldn't have gotten so excited, and now that she did, it isn't going to happen. I sit with her in this feeling and reflect that her grief is looking for something to control, so when she blames herself, she also obtains control. Rilee's self-blame and detachment represent protection because what is often misunderstood about this process is how much of your heart you sacrifice. Desiring an answer that sticks and doesn't change within hours because that information is directly tied to your heartstrings.

There is not only a seemingly unconscious effort in protection for herself, but in many ways, I saw her response as a protection for the child. Without even meeting this small, fresh-to-the-world infant, Rilee was already loving him, protecting him, and fighting for him. It has felt hard for her in the past to allow others in the pit of grief that she is in—a concept that is familiar to many. Somehow, our grief brain attempts to solve loneliness with isolation ... leading to more loneliness. It was tough for Rilee to even allow her husband in that pit with her, as there is a desire to be in the space and deal with it on her own. Other women might agree that the role of being a mother is a distinct and nonidentical experience than that of another caretaker, again, making our grief of that role more feel more isolating. To build tolerance and acquire perceived control, we mistakenly blame others or ourselves. I tell Rilee that though we can validate the self-blame is playing a role, it's not the truth, the truth being that as a foster parent, there is unfortunately little in your control, and you are a marionette attached to your heartstrings, played by external forces. If we can replace blame with compassion, might it be possible to have room for both how it feels and the truth? Rilee nods her head. "I can try."

I ask Rilee, "So, to answer your friends' question....Why do you do this to yourself? Why are you a foster parent?"

With tears in her eyes, she says, "Because I want to parent children who don't have anyone else to."

"Why is that important? Why is that worth the pain and sacrificing your heart?"

"So a child can feel cared for, loved, and safe."

14

Elephants

" **I**n 2019, I also lost my grandfather, who was beyond amazing. He was really the first loss I've experienced as an adult. He was ninety-four years [old], and I got to spend so much time with him, as he lived so close to me. I was extremely lucky for that. I grieve for him, but I know he's okay and happy to be reunited with my grandmother. Both experiences are completely opposites. I wish I could be as at peace with my dad's death as my grandfather's. The worst part is I feel bad for myself. I have no father figure in my life anymore. Back-to-back, I lost the most important men in my life. It's hard to think about the future—all the things they will miss in my life, the important life stages in my life."

Research participant, female, twenty-nine, Massachusetts

My grandmother, Selma "Rusty" Sokoll, passed away at the age of only sixty-eight on December 26, 1998. I was eight years old. She and my grandfather lived on Highcrest Road in Fall River, Massachusetts. My mom and my four other siblings were visiting, as we commonly did on winter break from school. On the morning of, my mom woke us all up so we could go to Building 19, a huge quirky warehouse of a discount store that had anything you could think of. My siblings and I had come to love this place, as it was a "trip to Grandma and Grandpa's house" must-see. My grandpa had already left for his day at the office, and just before we were about to leave, I opened the door to his and my grandma's bedroom and peaked my little head in. I saw my grandma sleeping and thought about waking her up to say goodbye and tell her where we were going. Maybe she wanted to come. But for some reason that I still don't know, I didn't. I shut the door and left the house to start the day of discount shopping fun.

When we would go to Building 19, we would load up on clothes, shoes, school supplies, snacks, maybe even a rug. Stocking up on things that we probably didn't need but we *couldn't live without it!* I liked going to the book section because it was massive, though every section of the store was massive. My mom would let each of the five of us get one "gift," something we could pick out for ourselves. The only thing I remember from that trip was thinking that I couldn't find anything I liked until I came upon a definitely-fake marble onyx small elephant figurine. I remember being pulled to it, instantly knowing this was what I wanted, and fit it into my small eight-year-old hand.

I don't have any memory of this, but we must have gone somewhere after because from what I recall, I was told that my grandpa had come home for his lunch break, like he did every day. When we got back to my grandma and grandpa's, there were numerous emergency vehicles with lights blaring outside the house. I fell asleep on the car ride home, though I was in a light daze because I remember discretely opening my eyes, seeing the chaos, closing my eyes, and pretending I was still asleep. "Waking up" by the commotion, performing a tired and sleepy character, I asked what was going on as if I had just discovered the scene. Twenty-three years later, I still have shame about this. To my recollection, until now, I had never shared that part of the story. I still can't say for sure why I did that. Clinically knowing what I know now, maybe I was protecting myself; if I pretended that I was asleep, I could avoid the emergency that was about to unfold. Maybe I wanted to focus on myself. I can see now that whatever the case may be, avoidance was certainly a part of it.

My mom parked the car in the driveway and ran into the house. The next-door neighbors who were friends with my grandparents opened the doors to our car and told us we were going to go play at their house. I remember being in their living room and playing with my new elephant, feeling like we had been there for *forever.* The last memory I have of that day is my mom bringing me and my older brother, Nathan, into the kitchen; the cantor from the synagogue was there. My grandma had died. When I recollect this as an adult, a vivid particularity that sticks out from the whole day is my mom holding Nathan and I in her arms, feeling her body rapidly yet delicately bounce up and down as the emotion was released. Each of us embraced by her arms, pulling us close to her, facing opposite ways. Not being able to see my mother's face made it unclear to decipher the emotion being displayed. I thought she was laughing. Up until that point in my life, that was the only expression of emotion my mom showed me that was familiar enough and resembled the sound and body movement she was making. Only when the embrace was lifted did I see her face. I had never seen my mom cry before. I couldn't identify it because I didn't know what it looked like, felt like. To be held in someone's arms while they cried— this was my first experience.

The elephant figurine has come in and out of my life since 1998. Frankly, I'm surprised I didn't lose it or forget it in Massachusetts when we eventually went back home to Maryland. Since the age of eight, the elephant has been displayed, covered, lost, and found. There were several years where I had no idea where it was, a casualty of a messy room or maybe a move to college. But eventually, it showed up again and was back in my life. Since that time, I have kept an eye on it. This small imitation marble onyx figurine is how my fascination with elephants began. Reminding me of the connection I have always had with my grandma and maybe the connection I have had since 1998 with grief. My grandma was the first human loss I remember experiencing, and my eight-year-old self didn't know how to cope. The loss and grief I felt were supremely impactful and different from how I perceived my siblings' or cousins' grief to be. The death of my grandma has always been a cardinal event in my life and in my narrative. Having elephants in my life has been a way for me to continue the relationship with my grandma. This connection and love were even more magnified on my trip to Thailand, where I went to Elephant Nature Park, a rescue and rehabilitation center. It was one of the most wholehearted, soul-feeding experiences of my life. Elephants have a sense of self, high emotional intelligence, and the ability to not only mourn death but console other elephants in distress. The protection I feel for elephants and my family is a similar protection to how my grandma felt for me and our family. Similar to a response from the research, my grandmother was the matriarch of our family. It's no surprise that elephant herds are also led by a strong matriarch. I hope to fulfill this role one day: succeeding my grandmother, mother, and aunt, and all the other matriarchal elephants in my life.

"Secondarily, losing my grandmother in January 2017. I chose to grieve in the moment and then block the fact that she been gone for two and a half years. She was the matriarch of our family and really the glue, and it is so hard to see the family without her, as it just isn't the same."

Research participant, female, thirty-one, Texas

Twenty-two percent of responses from the research describe the death of a grandparent. Of the individuals who describe the loss of something or someone specific, the loss of a grandparent was the most reported loss. Given that a large majority, seventy-eight percent, of the responses came from individuals under forty years old, it wasn't surprising to me that they shared this loss, as it is generally an expectation that by the time one is forty years old, grandparents may no longer be living. Even with this expectation, the loss of a grandparent can be devastating.

"My grandfather died in October, and my grandmother died in March. Losing grandparents is very overwhelming—way more than I thought. I had a very hard time when my grandmother passed away. My grandfather died right after my brother's wedding, and we delayed his memorial for some reason. Having to push away his death and then all of the sudden be confronted with it was scary."

Research participant, female, twenty-seven, New Jersey

"I had my first true experience with grief about two years ago when my grandpa passed. He was a huge part of my life. I didn't have a dad growing up, but Pops stepped in and filled that role. He was my protector, my stability, my supporter in everything I did. He was a man of few words, but he didn't have to say much to make you feel cared for.

Research participant, female, twenty-seven, Texas

"I lost my grandfather to cancer four years ago. He was probably the most important person to me, next to my mom....I miss his hand lotion. And how he dressed like he just got out of prison. And how when he wasn't living with me, he called at the same time daily, like when he was in prison lol. I miss how he kept all my secrets and knew me better than I knew myself. I miss his hugs. I miss how he would hold my hand and make me sandwiches and play with my hair because he knew it would make me fall asleep and keep me from going out and getting into trouble. I wish he didn't have to die."

Research participant, female, thirty-one, Maryland

For many people, there is a special bond with a grandparent. I have worked with quite a few people who were raised primarily by their grandparents, often having unique experiences from others whose primary caregivers were their parents. This seems to be especially true for people whose parents were still alive, though unable to care for their children for one reason or another. A client of mine had described the relationship with her dad to be like that of a brother. After the death of her grandfather, my client identified a role reversal with her father, finding herself in a role of the responsible parent to a dependent. The change in role after experiencing a death, especially of a family member, is a familiar undertaking for many. This can then evolve into a change and loss of identity for the individual, leaving us with responsibilities that we have never prepared for.

"I'm grieving as a caregiver. I lost my great-grandmother in August after being her direct caregiver for the past three years. It's been difficult because great-grandparents are supposed to die. I know I'm lucky to have had her for so long. Being the great-granddaughter made me removed, but yet as her caregiver, I saw her through the past few years. I also had to hold my family together because as a social worker, they just assume I can, and I do. I know grief is not linear. But I wish I could have grieved like a normal great-granddaughter and not the social work caregiver who now can finally feel emotions so many months later."

Research participant, female, twenty-seven, Maryland

"I lost my grandfather the day after I graduated college. My parents worked full-time when I was growing up, so my grandfather and grandmother got me to school, picked me up and fed me, and put me to bed for my whole childhood. My grandfather died June 1, and I started my first real job June 24. With my family working, I needed to be my grandmother's support system. I planned the funeral, handled Social Security, all of it. It has been eleven months since he has been gone, and it wasn't until I spent Easter in quarantine all by myself that it really hit me that he was gone. I was so busy taking

care of everyone else in my family that I
never dealt with my own grief. It hit me
like a cement wall. My chest was heavy.
Tears fell for the first time in a year. I
mourned that day for his life and my life
without him. This past year without him, I
have thought about him every day, but I
thought about getting my grandmother
'through this' more."

*Research participant, female, twenty-five,
New Jersey*

The expectation that we will outlive our grandparents takes the road of acceptance for some. There can be conflicting feelings with this, even judgement for handling the loss with limited pain and suffering. Knowing that the loss of a grandparent is upon us has the potential to make the emotions easier to cope with.

"At first, I wanted to talk about my
grandfather's death, which occurred three
months ago. But then, I realized that my
writing will be short because the truth is I
didn't observe any grieving. The reason why
[is] my grandfather was already dead to me.
This fact is not because I didn't love my
granddad, but quickly in the contest, he was
suffering from Alzheimer's. The disease
started to appear five years ago, and little
by little, it got worse. He spent his last
years and his last days of existence in a
specialized medical institute, which was a
release for my grandmother. I didn't cry

> when my mother called me to announce his
> death. I didn't feel any emotional pain so
> far. I remember; I was prepared. It made my
> grieving easier, I guess."
>
> *Research participant, feminine, Québec*

I was with my two siblings, Kyla and Jadon, when my grandpa, Francis "Fishy" Sokoll, died on November 29, 2019. They both came to visit me in Austin for Thanksgiving from their respective cities before I left a few days later to go to Australia, where my other two siblings, Nathan and Nediva, were living for the time being. The funeral was planned for the following week, and I felt conflicted on what I *should* do when I already knew what I *wanted* to do. It's somewhat rare to be with my siblings, because we have all lived or done extended travel in different places all over the country and world for many years. I knew Nediva and Nathan weren't going to make it back to the States from Australia for the funeral, and Kyla and Jadon were planning on changing their outbound flight from Austin, now heading to Massachusetts. I went to Australia. If I am being honest, I didn't want to experience another loss that I actually had control over. I spent a lot of money, took time from work, and was looking forward to not only seeing my siblings whom I had not seen in a long time but also going to a place that I had dreamt about going to for most of my life. Family was the most important thing to my grandpa, and going to my siblings when they could not come to us felt like a way I could honor him.

I didn't cry very much when my grandfather died. I don't remember feeling much of anything when my mom told me over the phone that he had passed away. For months, my family prepared as much as they could for the end of my grandpa's life. I went to Massachusetts to see him for what would end up being the last time for a weekend in September of 2019. I prepared for the possibility that it was going to be the last time by spending as much time as I could with him, recording conversations we had and asking him to tell stories. Having pictures and videos of him during that trip has made missing him easier, though I haven't felt much pain in the grief process. In fact, it almost doesn't even feel like a grief process, though maybe it's because I started grieving the loss of him years ago. I knew that this gregarious, joyful, light-up-the-room kind of guy was in the final act of his life. I felt gratitude for him passing before the rise of the pandemic. I recognize this as a gift, not having him experience the fear, grief, and loneliness that he would have if he had been alive. I felt lucky that my family didn't have to go through the possibility of him dying from COVID, as I saw many clients and friends experience this with their grandparents and older adults in their life.

The grief I have for the death of my grandfather is unlike any other grief I have experienced because it immediately showed up as gratitude. The love he showed to all his grandchildren was boundless and one of the greatest gifts of my life. I will continue to have sadness to never hear the words "Arielle my bell" in the most joyful and welcoming tone. I'll never stop missing him, never stop loving him. Wherever his soul might be, I hope it's a place where there are unlimited amounts of borscht, plenty of perfectly sunny beach days, and the Red Sox always win.

What It Means to be Alive

" I grieve for my country, my friends, my family, and all the other moments of my life that are now past.

"I grieve for my country because of its lost promise. I grieve for ideals of justice and compassion swallowed by greed and everyday meanness. I grieve for discourse and reason replaced by clever one-liners and the swill of slogans. I grieve for facts that have been replaced by lies. I grieve for conscience corrupted by unrestrained capitalism. I grieve for open-mindedness murdered by self-righteous delusion. I grieve for leaders who serve only their careers and exploit the people they should be serving. Any sense of shared purpose is dead.

"I grieve for my friends lost by time and distance and now death. The men I lived with in college, partied with, learned with, and discovered the mysteries and protocols of life [with] have disappeared into their own lives of drama, success, and in some cases, despair and suicide. I miss the camaraderie, the fun, the affirmation of those friends. Mourn the knowledge of the ones who have died, that I shall never see them again.

"I grieve for my mother, my father, my aunts and uncles, and my cousins who have passed away. Generations of relatives passing one by one. The people who, even if not close, were linked by a bond of blood. I remember summer Saturdays in a great farmhouse in upstate New York surrounded by grandparents, aunts, uncles, and cousins of every age and the sense of family known but so rarely experienced as an only child.

"I grieve for the heroes of my youth. Musicians young and beautiful as gods. Creators of sound and lyrics that transformed their generation and were the soundtrack of my life. Fewer and fewer survive with each year that passes.

"I hold on to memory because it is all that is left. I shall never again kiss my mother or my father. I shall never sit in my grandmother's kitchen again at a table with a red-checkered tablecloth and the smell of tomato sauce cooking on her stove. I shall never hear the dancing notes of Jerry's guitar or the buzz saw chords of "One Way Out." I shall never see another leader who can inspire a nation.

"Grief is about loss. The terrible loss of things that can never be again. Reverence

for the past can never replace it. Hold on
to the moment. It is all there is.

*Research participant, male, sixty-eight,
Vancouver*

Recognizing that that there is immense loss in life apart from death can be jolting. Impartially, we know it exits, though it can be difficult to recognize within ourselves and our own world. I tell my clients that we experience loss every day, from the car that swooped in and stole your Saturday morning long-hunted parking space to finding out your best friend is moving back to Ohio. We attach to these things, even if only for a brief moment. Attachment is a fundamental element in grief. Our attachment system, and the concluding grief that follows when the system is threatened by disconnection, is an extension of a course that has changed over time, so we as individuals feel as safe and prepared for survival as possible. When we experience a nondeath loss, this often involves the loss of a part of ourselves that we are attached to or our place in the world that creates a sense of security.[1] Examples are found in responses from the research:

"I think I'm learning to grieve about
different things in my life, not just death,
which is a new concept for me in the last
couple of years. Grieving concepts that I'm
realizing don't make sense ... grieving my
life not looking like I may have thought it
would."

*Research participant, female, twenty-eight,
Texas*

---

[1] Williams, "Disen-Whaaaat?? Understanding Disenfranchised Grief."

"I think grief presents in my life in multiple different facets.

"Grief in continuing to feel unaccepted and not achieving where I thought I would be at twenty-five. Grieving that I am known and fully loved by my community and my family, but I cannot ever accept it or rest in that knowledge.

"Grieving that maybe I have not reached full recovery from my eating disorder but unwilling to voice it.

"Grieving that the job that I thought I wanted my entire life I hate and grieving that I cannot find a new job in this season of pandemic, that I do not have enough experience yet, and that I have been looking for seven months and only have gotten one interview.

"Grieving that I have a hard time enjoying the present because some small aspects I am engaging with suck and all I can think about is getting away.

"Grieving that dating is hard for me. That I cannot get over past hurts/heartbreaks and how I have not been able to drop my baggage and trust fully someone else with my heart. That I constantly feel like I need to seek validation that he still loves me and that he is not talking or cheating behind my back. That I cannot get over a boyfriend's ex that he still loved at the beginning of our relationship.

"Grieving that I care more about what other people think about me rather than how I see myself or care about myself enough to go seek help.

"I feel grief that I don't care so much about my parents' divorce.

"I feel grief that I do not care about mending some relationships that were fruitful because I do not want to put in the energy."

Research participant, female, twenty-seven, Texas

The disequilibrium that occurs from these nondeath losses can activate our attachment, guiding us closer to the things we know are comfortable and familiar. The grieving process encourages us to then adapt to a new part of ourselves or a new part of our life that is now noticeably changed from before.[2] Even feeling grief for things that were never ours to begin with can feel distracting and impactful. This is disappointment: hoping and wishing for something that we do not have, though want to add to our life, then feeling the loss anyway. Our assumptive world, a concept from Ronnie Janoff-Bulman, refers to our core beliefs: the things that ground, stabilize and orient us in our world. When death and trauma are introduced to our world, these beliefs are demolished, and we are therefore left disoriented.[3] How we relate to the world, others, and ourselves is an extension of the attachment system that was formed at a very young age, suggesting that when our assumptive world is threatened, it

---

[2] Estroff Marano, "At a Loss."
[3] Beder, "Loss of the Assumptive World—How We Deal with Death and Loss."

evokes the attachment system where that world was originally created.[4]

Most of us walk around with living losses clinging on to us like a shy child. Living losses are ongoing losses that exist and intertwine with everyday life and generally are embraced by a category of nonfinite loss. Nonfinite losses are persistent and provoked by a negative life event that retains a physical and/or psychological continual existence. What could start out as a finite event might actually have consequences for a lifetime. Another example of nonfinite loss could be something less defined, though it leaves a sense of uncertainty and ongoing adjustment.[5]

"My grief comes from my cousin being on the first tour to Iraq and the government not knowing how to deal with PTSD when he came back."

Research participant, female, twenty-seven, New Jersey

"I think that grief runs on a spectrum and isn't necessarily an either-or emotion. I haven't had many deaths close to me, so I don't necessarily associate bereavement with grief. I have grieved loss of relationships with friends, family, and partners in the sense that I think about what went wrong and what could have been. I have grieved being rejected from jobs and colleges I really wanted. I've been diagnosed with major

---

[4] Estroff Marano, "At a Loss."
[5] Estroff Marano, "At a Loss."

> depressive disorder, so sometimes I'm not
> sure if what I'm feeling is grief or
> symptoms of my diagnosis. I know grief is
> supposed to be temporary in a sense, but I
> feel like my grief lasts longer but isn't as
> harsh over time."
>
> *Research participant, female, twenty-five,*
> *Texas*

Divulging into the ending of romantic relationships was significant within the research responses, and as one might imagine, often a topic that not only shows up in therapy but encourages someone to start therapy. I have had more conversations with more clients than I could count about the grief experienced when a relationship ends. It can feel like a soul-crushing setback that leads us to other experiences of grief and loss. Humans are social creatures, so much so that not only do we need contact and connection to thrive, but we need it to survive.

When we form an intimate connection and enter a relationship with another person (or people), and that relationship ends, we can experience symptoms of withdrawal. A relationship can be a literal chemical addiction, as the dopamine system is triggered during social or intimate interactions. This then activates and interacts with the oxytocin system and creates pair bond formation. When both systems are activated at the same time, social and reward aspects come together, forming not only a chemical bond but a relational one as well.[6] It's no wonder that a breakup or divorce often has such a long recovery period; we were more or less addicted to someone who has new retired from their main character role in our life. It's heartbreaking! In fact, we might even have broken heart syndrome ... seriously. Moving down from the brain to the heart, we can experience a rapid weakening of the heart muscle after sudden physical or emotional stress. This is called broken heart

---

[6] Young, "Dopamine, Oxytocin, Rewards, and Bonding."

syndrome. It mimics symptoms of a heart attack, but don't worry; it's a temporary and reversible heart condition also known as stress cardiomyopathy.[7] Similar to the distress we feel in grief: Painful? Yes. Permanent? Unlikely.

"The grief I felt from the breakup was from struggling with five years of having a fear of being lonely and becoming a person I that I didn't recognize (which means I stayed with him even though I knew what he was doing was wrong—because I was scared to be alone and did not form any connections with other people than him and being an angry person because I wanted him to be the person he was when he was sober). The grief I also felt was for myself for staying in the relationship as long as I have with how he treated me mentally, emotionally, and physically. It was the most taxing relationship I had ever been in, and I grieved because I felt I lost five years of my life to someone who didn't love or care for me to begin with."

Research participant, female, thirty-seven, Texas

---

[7] American Heart Association, "Is Broken Heart Syndrome Real?"

"Tomorrow ... would have been my eighth
anniversary with my partner. Our
relationship ended in February, at which
time I learned he had been seeing someone
else for eighteen months. Neither of us knew
about the other, and had a friend of mine
and a friend of hers not figured it out, the
lies probably would have continued. Most
people I've talked to don't seem to
understand how neither she nor I were
willing to walk away. We forced him to
choose. He did not choose me, and that was
probably the single most painful thing I've
ever experienced. One of the biggest parts
of my life was gone just like that. I had
cultivated a very independent life (lived in
another town, few shared property/accounts,
etc., not married, no kids), and so I was so
frustrated that this felt like such a loss
when I still had so much. I work at a job I
love, have amazing friends, and am a grad
student loving my program. How could I feel
like none of that matters, even for the
brief moments in time when it does? Our
relationship had issues and many things I
let go that I shouldn't have, but it's still
painful that a major part of my reality was
lost."

Research participant, female, thirty-two,
Texas

There were multiple research participants that shared living and nonfinite losses around moving locations and homes. The response below paints a vivid picture of how attachment systems are involved and consequently play out our experience with grief. The research participant shares her nonfinite losses that arose from moving from Melbourne to London:

"The deepest grief I experienced lately was in moving countries earlier this year, from Melbourne (Australia) to London (UK). The month leading up to the move involved an immense sense of 'letting go' of everything I know my life in Melbourne to look like. I have lived in Melbourne my entire life: My whole network of people is there. The home I grew up in was there. The first home I created for myself was there. My first jobs were there, etc. The weeks before leaving Melbourne, I felt like I was crying on the hour every hour. I kept thinking to myself, *I don't know when and if I do return to this place, but if I ever do return, it is not going to ever be the place that I left behind. Things will happen; people will move on, etc. My network of people will be fewer.* No matter how much people say, 'We will still be in touch,' there are just some people inevitably who you will lose touch with. I found this thought to be the hardest, knowing that I will be saying a last goodbye to some of the great people in my life right now. I was preemptively mourning their place in my life as it currently stands. My home will never be the same—I won't ever be moving back into my last share-house, where I had some of the greatest memories in my life. Hypothetically, even if I did move back, it would be different. Somebody else would have shared 'my space'; somebody else would have bonded with my roommates. This would be somebody else's home. Again, I was mourning this home, which was so great to me. I very deliberately wanted to say goodbye and mourn these elements of my life on my own terms and do it properly. So many of my friends have moved overseas for a period of time and end up mourning on their return, being shocked that life isn't as it was five years ago when they left. This always shocked me. Of course, it isn't going to be how you left it. People/cities/life/homes/jobs all move on without you. I hated the thought of leaving and not properly honoring the life that was good to me in Melbourne. Perhaps it made the whole leaving process more difficult than it had to be, but at the same time, I'm glad I'm not ignorant to the impact of this big 'change' to my life."

Research participant, female, thirty-one, London

Lucy*, another research participant, shares her experience retiring as a professional athlete at the age of twenty-seven, succeeding competing in the 2014 Winter Olympics. When describing her experience, Lucy tells me, "I lost so much, and I didn't even know it happened. It took time to realize I lost identity, structure, social connections, meaning, and hope." Sport was all she knew. It was not only her job; it became her life. Lucy was now without a map in a foreign place where sport was no longer the heart and center of her world and experiencing a complete loss of identity. "Losing identity is even more exaggerated [than other losses]; it can shake a person so much," she said. As previously discussed in the earlier chapter, the loss of identity can leave us feeling stuck, not knowing which way to go, as every direction has uncomfortable uncertainty. Lucy's assumptive world was shattered, and in order to rebuild, it would be necessary for her to grieve her losses that led to life changes and transitions—some in ways she never could have prepared for.

Grief is not only necessary for all of us, but it is also adaptive in order to reassemble the assumptive world after the shattering. Opportunely, this helps the meaning-making part of the grief response that benefits both death- and nondeath-related losses.[8]

---

[8] Estroff Marano, "At a Loss."

16

Waiting for the Exhale

"I wrote something once, about grief, that still rings true almost twenty years after Jeffrey's death:

Grief is a strange beast

Whenever I think it's nocturnal

It springs forth on me during daylight hours

During all hours.

I'm better today because of my grief. Not because I ignore it but because I embraced it, and I wrestled it, and I turned the beast into something much more submissive."

Research participant, female, thirty-one, Maryland

We heal best when we are given the opportunity to heal. When others ask how we are doing—and actually want to know. When we give ourselves the time and patience to be curious about our emotions and our thought process. When those in our support system make the physical and emotional space for vulnerability to be welcomed with open arms. When our environment is encouraging, and if we choose, giving ourselves permission to make room for who or what we lost in our life the way it looks now. Healing doesn't always show up, nor is it always welcomed soon after a loss. It could be late to the party ... sometimes *very* late to the party. If there is present healing, that means there is something to heal from. Reaching out to the grieving friend, especially when it's been years since the loss occurred, is sometimes what continues to get them through the tough days that still arise. They haven't forgotten about their loss. Show them that you haven't, either.

After a loss, especially the death of a loved one, it isn't unusual to feel afraid that you will experience another loss. We will think into the future and get stuck on the "what if" triggers that appear in our life. I have seen this in not only myself but many people I have worked with. For example, Carlyn* started coming to therapy after the death of her brother. She told me that she got the news about his death via phone call. Carlyn describes an "unreasonable fear of losing someone else," often playing graphic and generally unrealistic scenarios in her head about the death of another person in her life. When she gets a phone call from a family member that she wasn't expecting, or when the daily phone call from her mother doesn't come on time, this will often be a haunting trigger.

What is less understood is the fear of celebration or good things happening after we have endured loss. This might be surprising for some, as the pain that accompanies grief is so unpleasant; why wouldn't feeling better be desired? Being afraid of not only the good in life disappearing but especially the people we care most about. There can be a fear that we might not be strong enough to handle even a minor loss of something or someone we care about, so disengaging in the things that bring joy feels safer. To echo earlier chapters, having reservations about deserving celebration, humor, or joy is often a collective experience for mourners. As I tell my clients, "You are a human being. Therefore, you deserve happiness." I assure them that my job is not to convince people of things—ha, could you imagine?! And that they will smile again, laugh when something is too funny not to, and one day, someday, smile in gratitude when thinking about the person who left the party too early.

The odyssey of healing can take various routes, often getting lost and turned around a few times along the way. I think of my clients as though they are infants new to the world after a loss. Opening their eyes to a world that may seem a little darker and duller and unable to communicate in the way they want. Wanting and even expecting themselves to be more prepared and ready to continue a life that is now deeply changed. I hear this in what I call the "silent just." We are all too familiar with this: I just need to tell her how I feel; I just need to wake up earlier; I just need to accept it; I just need to figure it out on my own.

To all of these and more, I jokingly say to my clients: *Oh! What a great idea! That should be pretty easy, right?*

No matter how much grief I go through, my sass will never die.

Why is it the *silent* "just," you might be wondering? Because we don't seem to hear the reason why we use the word. If "needing to accept it" was so easy, wouldn't you already be doing it? The "just" dismisses the hardship that is blatantly there and replaces it with a judgmental expectation of ease. It also encourages us to hustle through this challenge, loss, or hardship we are experiencing because, let's face it, we got shit to do. Acknowledging the transitions that take place at an undisclosed speed can feel intolerable. Therefore, the "silent just" is a way to convey our avoidance.

To be living with loss and grief means that with every one of these transitions we go through when healing, as well as the various transitions when we continue to live our lives, we adjust to new truths. Be it new relationships, moving to a new place, or getting a new job, we must adjust to the truth that a person we cared for deeply is not physically here to be with us in the transition. This is a testament to how grief shifts but is never extinct. My client Zayne once brought up in a session how the grief "process" makes us think that it is something that we be continuously worked on all the time. I agreed; the use of the work, "process" makes it seem like there is an ending, as well. As if we get through the process and then we can check it off the to-do list. Zayne shares a reframe: "Make it feel like a part of every process." By inviting the emotions of our grief into different parts of life, it can help us feel connected to what we grieve, acknowledge the distance that the loss spread across our life, and permit ourselves to take grief as slowly as we need to.

In a session with Audree, she told me that it was important to "release my intention on the outcome." This was in relation to how we often pretend we have a magic ball, looking into the future and being sure that what we think will happen will actually happen. Only wanting to do things or feel things if we know for sure they will bring us what we desire and intentionally fulfill our narrative. Thus, potentially holding us back from something that could bring us great relief or insight, just by having and engaging in that process.

The following is an excerpt from an interview with a research participant in his late sixties living in California. He shares with me a life-changing and very unique experience participating in EMDR over a decade ago, three years after the sudden death of his mother.

April 2, 2007, my mother was killed walking in a crosswalk. My mother was walking two steps ahead of my father. She was killed; he was not touched. So, it was a rather traumatic situation. My mother and I were extremely close, so it was a very, very tough blow. I got two phone calls. The first phone call was that "Grandma had been in an accident," and the second phone call was that she had died. I walked around with that for a couple of years. Then it was actually suggested that grief counseling would be a good idea. When I went into the grief counseling, they suggested EMDR....I did two sessions of EMDR, and the first session was a total strikeout....when I approached the second session, I had very low expectations for anything ... and what happened the second time was one of the most phenomenal experiences of my lifetime. It was an unbelievable experience. It became this very deep and moving experience....it was the most unbelievably intense experience. They would stop at various points and ask how I was doing, and I came to realize that tears were just pouring down my face ... my shirt was soaked. As they were going back in, it kept getting deeper and deeper, and as I was going through the course of that, I was actually able to see my mother's body in the road and get to a place of peace with it; I had not allowed my mind to imagine the scene [before that], but I was able to go there. My mother was talking to me and telling me that she knew that I had thought she had abandoned me, but she had not, that she was still there and still keeping an eye, and all was well....I told [the facilitator] that I'd really like to hold my mother. So, I went back into it, and I had the absolute sensation of holding my mother. I know this all sounds like crazy shit, but it could not have been more real. A couple of years before my mother was killed, my aunt had died; my mother's sister....she was like a second mother to me. At the end of the session, my aunt then appeared with my mother, and they said, *you're okay, everything is fine, we're here, you're good, we're good,* and then they turned to walk away, and it was like, almost cartoonish, and watching them walking and their figures getting smaller and smaller as they are walking into the distance....the two of them were talking and laughing, exactly how they did in life. They seemed very content with each other. Then, the session ended, and I've got to tell you, there was not one scintilla of dry clothing on me. It was an amazing outpouring of emotion. When I went back to the therapist ... I was in the middle of telling him when I stopped myself, and I said, 'I realize I was in a state of peace that I had a sense of physical and emotional tranquility that I had not felt in three years.' I've heard the word serenity in my life, as something to aspire to. That moment was when I came to understand what the word serenity meant.

It can be quite impressionable when there is a similar impact to our lives from the healing after a loss as there was when we endured the loss itself. When grieving, my client Audree has said, "You can either be grateful or entitled." In a way, one might say that we bounce back and forth between these two: wishing for a linear process *and* learning that isn't the case. Finding gratitude when reflecting on our loss provides permission for healing, something that most find a hard gift to give themselves. By coming to therapy to explore and process the losses, Audree started to and continues to mourn. She explains, "I didn't think I was going to have the opportunity for new skills to be learned, especially after all the surgeries....it now cracks a ceiling for me when there wasn't an impetus for it, no reason, no push, and no safety." Finding the language for an experience, thought, or feeling that we were previously unable to communicate to ourselves or others is a radical relief. Audree has graciously told me that through our therapeutic processes, I have helped her articulate what she can't, agreeing that it brings her substantial relief when the language is found. Audree shares, "It's so devastating when I can't communicate to someone else where I'm coming from or what I'm feeling. So, I keep trying and trying, hoping the words will come. I just want to be understood."

There's reasonable difficulty in giving ourselves permission and not being afraid to connect with grief. Yet, when this is postponed for very long, there is a significant stall in not only our healing but a loss of opportunity to emotionally be with and connect to the one we lost. I am reminded of this by a young client named Lisa*, whose mother passed away when Lisa was twenty years old. Now twenty-five years old, we started therapy together after the very recent loss of her father. She reflects, "I lost years of my life pushing [my mom's] memory away because I didn't want to deal with it and the emotions." Lisa reveals how, through embracing memories of her father and single-handedly creating and organizing a beautiful memorial service, she now knows her dad differently and gains a feeling of closeness that was desired since his death.

It was two months after Lisa's father had quickly and suddenly passed away from coronavirus when I met her. She was calm for the first session, giving me what I call the "elevator talk" of her life. Sharing the big events and therapy essentials one would figuratively check off a list of disclosure for a first session. Intellectualizing the loss rather than feeling it, Lisa was thrown into a business side of grief that many people do not realize even exists, including financials and property soon needing to be attended to. The legal responsibilities that were thrown into Lisa's world created a huge barrier for her to grieve the death of her father. She would often talk about not feeling seen or heard by other family members that were of minimal assist. Feeling like she and her struggle were invisible, Lisa felt like she was only viewed in the role that was unreasonably put on her by the family. Lisa continued to adopt and adapt to the role of always taking responsibility, as it has become instinct for her to accommodate others, feeling like everyone else is more important. Challenging this has been a difficult task at times, as Lisa would often struggle to trust her own judgement and often feel *betrayed* by her own being.

Even when participating in grief group therapy, Lisa would wonder, *is my grief big enough? Do I belong here?* Comparing ourselves to others is inevitable and normal. At the same time, it often leads to negative self-talk and invalidation. Lisa would compare her grief to others in the group and would feel "too stable to talk" because she was "on top of her chaos." Together, we were able to identify the shame Lisa felt, as she was "really good at 'being strong.'" She had never been given the space to be anything else, which led her to minimize a lot about herself and her experiences, especially in grief. Like a sponge, absorbing others' emotions, it took time, reflection, and processing to not only acknowledge but believe that Lisa was worthy of her grief and all the emotions that came with it.

In one session, Lisa gave herself the permission to get in touch with her anger and resentment towards her parents and towards both of their untimely deaths at such pivotal times in her life. Reflecting on the past and "the beautiful life they wrecked," there wasn't time to process their divorce and the loss of family around her. She grieved the life that she will never have: "My life was stolen; my identity was stolen."

Lisa's grief ebbed and flowed through the waves of the ocean of loss. Her reflection along the way was insightful and rewarding to hear. Though it didn't come easily, Lisa took monumental steps in challenging the role and narrative that she lived under because she saw that there was a valuable and attainable other option—and she found it in Hawaii.

One of my favorite things about doing this work is learning and seeing the people who my clients have lost through their eyes. I learned from Lisa that Hawaii was her father's oasis, and he taught her to "always have something to look forward to." She and her partner were about to go on a trip that was planned, pushed back, and way overdue. The session that Lisa and I had upon her return was nothing short of sensational, as she shared how she allowed herself to be present, let go of worry, and never once felt like she didn't deserve it. "I was just 'Lisa,'" she said. When telling me how coming home was difficult and sad, she also allowed herself to gain perspective of all the truly incredible things she has done in the past year. She validated, "I don't know anyone else who could have done this." This trip was clearly what Lisa needed, and deserved, to gain self-validation and compassion for the tireless energy and work she put in to support her family and take on the premature responsibilities life had handed her.

As mid-summer came, the first anniversary of her father's death and his birthday in synchronicity was upon her. Watching Lisa speak about her pride towards the beautiful day she had put together for her father was heartwarming. She called it an "I-got-you moment....It's the last way I can show my dad I really know him ... the last way to publicly honor him." It was beautiful to finally hear the self-love and forgiveness that had been absent for so long when she described going through old pictures of her family to include in the memorial service. Lisa warmly stated, "I don't have regrets about anything. I was a great daughter, and we were best friends."

When Lisa was in our therapy session following the weekend of the memorial, she came in saying she was still "riding the high," describing the memorial and time spent with her family as "the moment of unity we have been looking for" and the final things she got to do with her father. The light was radiating through Lisa in a way that seemed familiar to her, welcoming it back into her life. The highlight of the day, she said, was presenting the speech she wrote to the three hundred-plus people in attendance to celebrate her father's life. Lisa graciously read the speech to me in our session, to which I can truthfully say I have never cried so much as a therapist. Painting the picture of how she was inspired and vulnerable, Lisa called this the most beautiful weekend of her life. Thinking about the future and seeing her ability to take on the impossible, while still knowing she doesn't always have to, Lisa felt refueled to be a therapist after the loss of her dad. She has shared this dream with me before, and it makes me proud to know that someday (if not already) she will help others get through their grief and their hills in life. By owning her story, she will help others own theirs. On multiple occasions, Lisa has described how we are all mosaics of the people we admire the most; it is indisputable that her mother and father will continue to live on within her, far past their deaths.

17

"A Beautiful Life is Obtainable"

" I felt like I was untethered from reality— free floating in a wave of emotions that I had no idea how to deal with. At the same time, patients of mine started dying. I shut down completely. I felt nothing. And then, it all came back. Every time someone died, I questioned God; I got mad at God; I felt the grief of everyone else that had died. Over the years, friends and patients were dying from overdoses. And while at first, I shut down, I then learned to cope. To feel. To deal. To heal. I leaned into my pain. I wrote about it, talked about it, cried about it. And now, while patients and friends are still dying, I carry their memory with me. I carry Drew with me. I use my grief to motivate my truth and my service to others."

Research participant, female, thirty, Maryland

The title of this last chapter comes from Lisa's father. The words "a beautiful life is obtainable" represent a lived-out belief of his and something he encouraged Lisa and her sister to seek out and embrace as well.

Since graduating college from Towson University in 2013, I've had the opportunity to professionally speak in a variety of settings, including the college classroom. Professor Gold, who taught family law, was easily one of the best teachers I've had in any classroom. Continuing to stay in touch with him after graduation, I was grateful to have had a down-to-earth, intelligent, and legitimately cool person as a teacher. He not only made school fun but also demonstrated the importance of embracing life. It was Professor Gold who gave me my first speaking opportunity when I was invited to speak to his class about applying to grad school and my internship experience in my program at Towson and in my graduate program at University of Maryland School of Social Work. Before the start of the pandemic, I still was coming back to Towson University to the liberal arts building to talk to a room full of students. However, since 2013, the spoken narrative has changed, just as my life has. When I got sick in 2014, I started to talk about the concept of what happens when life doesn't go as planned. After Drew died in 2015, it turned into what happens when shit hits the fucking fan and how to make the choice to find resilience within yourself. The overarching theme was made clear: how do you become resilient, and how do you continue to stay resilient? What I wasn't aware of in 2015, and definitely not in 2013, was that talking about and owning my personal resilience was going to become a principal part of the rest of my life narrative.

Communities and individuals are innately resilient. We all have this superpower, though I have seen some people more than others struggle to rise to the occasion. According to George Bonanno, there is an identified mindset that characterizes individuals who adapt to loss without completely flattening: they are optimistic. Their challenge appraisal allows them to say, "Okay, this happened to me, and it is incredibly painful. But what do I need to do to get past this and survive?" They have coping skills that help them self-regulate and are used with a certain amount of flexibility. This flexibility is even seen on brain scans. First and foremost, however, the individual engages with the stressful event. The combination of optimism, challenge appraisal, and confidence in their coping mechanisms all sum up the process of what Bonanno calls "flexibility mindset."[1]

Acceptance of death is also a large part of a successful outcome when talking about resilience. Revisiting the role of identity in the grief process, people who are very dependent on the relationship with the deceased for their identity have challenges grieving the loss because there is a significant loss of identity in themselves when the other person dies. We generally see more successful outcomes of resilience when we can identify other aspects of our identity that help us continue on.[2] A common illustration of this is the identity of being a pet owner. Pets are one of the most effective protective factors. I have seen this validated time and time again with people of all ages and various demographics in my professional career thus far. Our identity of being this animal's main and sometimes only source of survival and affection literally saves human lives—and, at times, the animal's life as well.

This would be a great example of when I would introduce parts language in the therapeutic process. Janina Fisher, Ph.D. notes how important befriending emotional and body responses to trauma can be. Understanding ourselves as fragmented "parts," and therefore using part language, is a helpful way to not only better observe our somatic and emotional experiences but also enlist compassion within ourselves.[3] A couple of examples come to mind when I think about times when I have modeled parts language to a client: "It sounds like a part of you died when you lost your wife, and other parts continue to live on in your role as a mother and an athlete"; "a part of you is in so much pain knowing that you will never see your grandmother again. And another part of you feels relief that she is no longer in pain from her illness"; "though your husband died, you keep a part of him alive by talking to him every day."

---

[1] Estroff Marano, "At a Loss."

[2] Estroff Marano, "At a Loss."

[3] Prengel, "Janina Fisher: Integrating somatic approaches to trauma with 'parts' language."

As it has been overwhelmingly stated, after a loss, we can feel a part of ourselves missing. That part is precious and will always be missed, *and* we can remember that there are other parts that make us who we are. Embracing that flexibility allows us to effectively manage our expectations of the grief process and its habit of changing course. There is a freedom in managing what you can and releasing what you can't. A focus on what you can control and what you can change allows you to feel grounded. Learning to function now scored with a painful void will of course make it difficult to adjust, *and* this adjustment will come in phases as you learn how to come back to yourself and back to your power.

No one is going to take care of you like you. And yet, as a therapist, I am often pointing out and validating the skills and resources that clients already have and use that they are unable to see in the moment. It makes me wonder about the paradox of not wanting to give up the pain we feel because we have assigned meaning to it. We also then assign untrustworthiness to the thought of having the ability to survive the pain we feel and get to a place of healing. Psychologist Daniel Gilbert's work on affective forecasting addresses why people who are not in the therapeutic field may be suspicious of believing that they have their own resilience. When we are in a state of extreme discomfort or pain, it's difficult to imagine ourselves not being in that pain.[4] Being told that everything will be okay can feel super annoying or utterly wrong when we are hurting like hell. For example, in a session with a client who is grieving, I do my best to hold space for the hurt, validate the hurt, and give them space for that hurt. I also tell them that they will not hurt forever and that one day, things will feel easier.

Telling a client that they will survive this, that they have support, and that it won't always be the only thing they think about helps them engage with the stressor and their innate resilience. This is of course hard to tolerate, yet acknowledging and thinking about our grief is crucial. Asking ourselves questions about our current state and figuring out how to manage the moment. Asking ourselves, *what am I feeling right now? What about now? Have I ever felt like*

---

[4] Estroff Marano, "At a Loss."

this before? What skill can I use right now? I have done hard things before. I am resilient, and I will survive this.[5]

"Little by little, my sky started to be more
  blue, the grass started to be more green,
and I started to relisten to the birds. That
   was my way to acceptance. A new me was
  coming, full of confidence and trust. To
calm down all the negative thoughts flooding
into my brain, I worked hard to learn how to
 be grateful to myself and with the others.
    Despite my little rancor against
masculinity, I decided to see the light into
 people instead of darkness. I believe that
the way you think can have a major impact to
your life. Once we calm the mess who lives
   inside us, the outside world became more
joyful. All my grieving experiences actually
   allowed me to be stronger and more
confident, and I guess I wouldn't be the one
     I am now without them."

Research participant, feminine, Québec

Life comes with loss. We can, and must, allocate time to lean into sorrow and sadness, anger, and anguish. This is how we fire up resilience and how we find our strength. I recently came across a short yet powerful blog post written by Kent Thune about the paradox of death. There were a handful of details in the post that spoke to me, though the following quote really hit my heart:

---

[5] Estroff Marano, "At a Loss."

And so, we have two experiences that ultimately underscore The Paradox of Death: Death not only gives meaning to life, but it also is the enabler of life. The proximity to death equals the proximity to life; embrace death and you will live more fully. Today is your funeral. What did you miss?[6]

I've found that increasing tolerance to discomfort encompasses the goal of therapy. When we learn tolerance, we find resilience. Thune's quote encourages us to look at death, grief, and loss right in the face, because simply, it is a major part of life and something we do not have to fear. Resiliency does not mean going back, but instead, getting back up. Grief is a weird thing; it changes us deeply and personally, relationally and emotionally. When embraced, a very full life is possible.

"I started swimming again, on my own, and Jeffrey's suicide became the catalyst to my career as a mental health social worker, my involvement in suicide postvention research, my work with children and adults experiencing suicidal ideation and crises. I like to think that we shape our own destinies when it comes to grief. We lose a lot, but when we feel ready, we can take the loss and make meaning out of it."

Research participant, female, thirty-one, Maryland

---

[6] Thune, "The Paradox of Death."

Epilogue:

"I Am Living a Life Beyond My Wildest Dreams"

Drew was an active advocate in the Alcoholics Anonymous community. He was a voice that resonated with many and showed compassion to many more. Drew told me that others found solace in his words when he shared his own story because he was honest about his past and became an example of what you could be even when you were "one of the worst."

I only heard him share his story at an AA meeting one time. He made it look effortless, emptying his past and the struggles that brought him to the present. Drew communicated this in a way that didn't feel like an impingement and instead conveyed with poise.

He ended by saying,

"I am living a life beyond my wildest dreams."

It has stuck with me ever since. On multiple occasions, he would say that in the past, he was just living to die, that he had no respect for himself or his life, and it was a miracle he was alive today.

Hearing him profess that his life was more than he ever could have imagined was a joy to witness and privilege to be a part of.

That is what I admired about him then and continue to admire about him now:

His positivity, perseverance, and commitment to helping others.

Since his death, I am privileged to do everything I can to embody Drew's positivity, perseverance, and commitment to helping others. I take with great responsibility the serendipitous role that I am in as someone who has found the other side of grief. As I often tell my clients, I wish there was a magic wand I could flick to offload the pain experienced when a loss occurs, and there isn't. Instead, it oftentimes takes an unknown stretch of time that ruffles us in ways we couldn't have imagined and gives us choices along the way: stay idle or keep going. I do my very best—knowing that my best looks different every day—to be an example of what life can be when you choose the work of staring your grief in the face, being scared as hell with tears streaming down your face, and not knowing what is on the other side of this, but doing a

1, 2, 3, go and finding out.

Because to me, being *afraid* is not a good enough reason not to do something.

I kept going, and I have now found a life beyond my wildest dreams. Remember that although grief can be cyclical, healing is too. *Let your hurt save someone else.* So, choose to do the work, and keep going. Your wildest dreams are right in front of you.

Acknowledgements

I feel profoundly lucky to have so many people in my life who have inspired and encouraged me throughout the writing process and creation of this book. I would like to thank the following people:

My parents, Allison Sokoll and Bob Ward

My siblings, Nathan, Kyla, Nediva, and Jadon

Drew's family, Kathy, Steve, and Brad Weston, and the extended Weston family

My aunt and cousin, Rochelle Sokoll and Maya Sobel

The people who mentored and professionally inspired me, Saman Akhtar, Peter Olthoff, Carl Gold, Rick Levinson, Steve Moraco, Dr. Monique Walker, Mikki J. Gates, Rev. Erika Allison, Reno Gomez, Danielle E. Cochran, and Jordan Edelheit

My first grief therapist, Dr. Erin Stoll

My publisher, Inara Publishing, and Darren Slade, Ph.D.

Drew's chosen family, Jamie Nocher, Jack Devlin, and Digges Bosley

And with so much gratitude, my friends, Denise Williams and Jeffrey Williams, Erinn Smith, Thabita Senra, Brittany Smith and Grandpa, Shane Litts, Hannah Rose, Catherine Henning, Lauren Leon, Shauna Volpe, Danielle Polland, Michelle and Kyle Kordan, Kimmy Kagen, Nick Jameson, Adee Levinstein, Mallory

Ashwander, Devin Brown, Michaela Kornberg, Annette Toro, Walter Bentsen and Tom Bentsen, Kelly Hanrahan, Taylor Maurer, Tori Stoute, Ivy Le, Jen Dulski, Amanda Pannell Holtz, Sonya Villegas, Angela Suchon

Thank you for encouraging me and cheering me on. Thank you for sticking around and showing up, even when I tried to push you away. Thank you for answering the phone when I would call at 4:00 a.m. Thank you for listening when I was stressed and would bitch. Thank you for calling me out and naming things when I couldn't see them. Thank you for creating safe spaces for me. Thank you for being my friend, for loving me, and mentoring me.

My clients:
Thank you for allowing me a glimpse into your life. It is a privilege to walk with you in your grief, in your trauma, on your easy days and on the most excruciating ones. You bring meaning to not only my work as a therapist but also my life in a way that is beyond lucid comprehension. Thank you for trusting me with your vulnerabilities in an effort to help others. Your struggle, progress, and courage are an honor to witness.

The research participants:
Thank you for being so willing to share what so many try to hide. Thank you for demonstrating the complex makeup of grief by including your pain, humor, heartbreak, and relief. Be kind to yourself in the ongoing grief process.

New Zealand:
Thank you for bringing me back to life.

Bibliography

American Heart Association. "Is Broken Heart Syndrome Real?" American Heart Association. Accessed July 13, 2021. https://www.heart.org/en/health-topics/cardiomyopathy/what-is-cardiomyopathy-in-adults/is-broken-heart-syndrome-real#.WNhJbxLyvnU.

American Psychiatric Association, ed. "Trauma and Stressor Related Disorders." In *Diagnostic and Statistical Manual of Mental Disorders*. 5th ed, 271–80. Arlington: American Psychiatric Association, 2013.

Bananno, George, Laura Goorin, and Karin Coifman. "Sadness and Grief." Edited by Michael Lewis, Jeannette Haviland-Jones, and Lisa Feldman Barrett. Dissertation, Guilford Publications, 2010.http://personal.kent.edu/~kcoifman/publications_files/2 008_Bonanno,_Goorin,___Coifman_HANDBOOK_OF_EM OTION.pdf.

Beder, Joan. "Loss of the Assumptive World—How We Deal with Death and Loss." *OMEGA - Journal of Death and Dying* 50, no. 4 (June 2005): 255–265. doi:10.2190/GXH6-8VY6-BQ0R-GC04.

Black Lives Matter Global Network Foundation Inc. "About." Black Lives Matter. December 16, 2020. https://blacklivesmatter.com/about/.

Bluck, Susan, Eryn J. Newman, and D. Stephen Lindsay. "False memories: What the hell are they for?" *Applied Cognitive Psychology* 23, no. 8 (November 2009): 1105–1121. doi:10.1002/acp.v23.

Dazzi, T., R. Gribble, S. Wessely, and N. T. Fear. "Does asking about suicide and related behaviours induce suicidal ideation? What is the evidence?" *Psychological Medicine* 44, no. 16 (December 2014): 3361–3363. doi:10.1017/S0033291714001299.

DelGaudio, Derek. *In & Of Itself.* Hulu, 2021. www.hulu.com/movie/derek-delgaudios-in-of-itself.

DeRose, Natalie. "Avoidance Versus Distraction: Which One Are You Doing?" Toronto Psychologists. Accessed May 4, 2021. https://www.torontopsychologists.com/avoidance-versus-distraction.

Ellis, Linda. "Dash Poem: Live Your Dash: Poem about Life: Funeral Poem." The Dash Poem, September 1, 2020, https://thedashpoem.com/. Accessed 9 February 2020.

Estroff Marano, Hara. "At a Loss." Psychology Today. June 19, 2020. www.psychologytoday.com/us/articles/202006/loss.

Haley, Eleanor. "Types of Grief: Yes, there's more than one." What's Your Grief. April 16, 2020. https://whatsyourgrief.com/types-of-grief/.

Hand, Cynthia. *The Last Time We Say Goodbye.* Reprint ed. HarperTeen, 2016.

Healthwise Staff. "Depression." Premier Health. September 23, 2020.https://www.healthwise.net/premierhealth/Content/StdDocument.aspx?DOCHWID=hw30709.

Herbert, Wray. "Mourning and Memory: A Paradoxical Grief." Association for Psychological Science. January 11, 2013. https://www.psychologicalscience.org/news/were-only-human/mourning-and-memory-a-paradoxical-grief.html..

Katz, Dara. "Knowing the Difference between Primary and Secondary Emotions Could Be the Key to Fighting Fairly with Your Partner." PureWow. September 10, 2020. https://www.purewow.com/wellness/primary-and-secondary-emotions#:~:text=Thomas%20says%20that%20primary%20emotions..

Kubler-Ross, Elisabeth. *On Death and Dying.* New York: Macmillan Pub. Co., 1969.

Lawrence, Lawrence, Keith, Stacey Sutton, Anne Kubisch, Gretchen Susi, and Karen Fulbright-Anderson. *Structural Racism and Community Building Pdf.* Washington DC: Aspen Institute Roundtable on Community Change, 2004. https://www.aspeninstitute.org/wp-content/uploads/files/content/docs/rcc/aspen_structural_racism2.pdf.

National Institute for the Clinical Application of Behavioral Medicine. "How to Work with the Traumatized Brain." Training Program. *NICABM*, 2020. https://www.nicabm.com/confirm/trauma-vdk/.

Otgaar, Henry, Peter Muris, Mark L. Howe, and Harald Merckelbach. "What Drives False Memories in Psychopathology? A Case for Associative Activation." *Clinical Psychological Science* 5, no. 6 (November 2017): 1048-69. doi:10.1177/2167702617724424.

Paperny, Tanya. "Do Some Trauma Survivors Cope by Overworking?" *The Atlantic*, February 19, 2017. https://www.theatlantic.com/health/archive/2017/02/do-some-trauma-survivors-cope-by-overworking/516540/..

Pederson, Lane, and Cortney Sidwell Pederson. *The Expanded Dialectical Behavioral Therapy Skills Training Manual: Practical Dbt for Self-Helf and Individual.* Eau Claire: Premier Publishing and Media, 2012.

Prengel, Serge. "Janina Fisher: Integrating somatic approaches to trauma with 'parts' language." Relational Implicit. Accessed August 16, 2021. https://www.relationalimplicit.com/fisher-janina-parts/.

Robin, Diangelo. "White Fragility." *International Journal of Critical Pedagogy* 3, no. 3 (2011): 54.

Selzer, Leon. "What your anger may be hiding." Psychology Today. July 11, 2008. https://www.psychologytoday.com/us/blog/evolution-the-self/200807/what-your-anger-may-be-hiding.

Shpancer, Noam. "Laws of Emotional Mastery." *Psychology Today*, May 1, 2021.

Tenny, Steven, Grace D. Brannan, Jannelle M. Brennan, and Nancy C. Sharts-Hopko. "Qualitative Study." PebMed. May 30, 2021. https://pubmed.ncbi.nlm.nih.gov/29262162/.

Thune, Kent. "The Paradox of Death." *The Financial Philosopher* (blog), 2011. thefinancialphilosopher.com/2011/05/the-paradox-of-death.html.

Toro y Moy. *Freelance*. Washington DC: Carpark Records, 2019. https://www.youtube.com/watch?v=FlvP5vBlkTQ.

Wagner, Dee. Member Insights: Polyvagal Theory in Practice. *Counseling Today*, June 27, 2016.
https://ct.counseling.org/2016/06/polyvagal-theory-practice/.

Williams, Litsa. "Cumulative Grief aka Grief Overload Aka 'holy Crap I Can't Handle All This Loss'!!!" What's Your Grief. April 16, 2020. https://whatsyourgrief.com/cumulative-grief-aka-grief-overload/.

————. "Disen-Whaaaat?? Understanding Disenfranchised Grief." What's Your Grief. June 17, 2020. https://whatsyourgrief.com/disenfranchised-grief/..

————. "Guilt and Grief: Coping with the Shoulda, Woulda, Couldas." What's Your Grief. April 12, 2017. https://whatsyourgrief.com/guilt-and-grief-2/.

————. "Secondary Loss -- One Loss Isn't Enough??!!" What's Your Grief. April 16, 2020. https://whatsyourgrief.com/secondary-loss-one-loss-isnt-enough/.

YW Boston. "What Is Intersectionality, and What Does It Have to Do with Me?." *YW Boston Blog. YWCA Boston*, April 25, 2018. ywboston.org/2017/03/what-is-intersectionality-and-what-does-it-have-to-do-with-me/.

Young, Larry. "Dopamine, Oxytocin, Rewards, and Bonding." DNA Learning Center. Accessed August 3, 2021. https://dnalc.cshl.edu/view/2384-dopamine-oxytocin-rewards-and-bonding.html.

Your Family Entertainment. "Air Bud." Vimeo Video. *Vimeo*, February 10, 2015. https://vimeo.com/119243332.

CPSIA information can be obtained
at www.ICGtesting.com
Printed in the USA
LVHW020713160222
711266LV00008B/423